PYTHON

PROGRAMMING FOR CYBER SECURITY WITH SCAPY AND IMPACKET

A Practical Guide to Master Network Security, Ethical Hacking and Penetration Testing

Jade L. Rhodes

1

Table of Contents

Part 1: Introduction to Cybersecurity and Python

Chapter 1: Introduction to Cybersecurity

Hey there, future cyber guardians! You've picked up this guide, and that tells me you're ready to explore the fascinating intersection of Python programming and network security. Get ready to wield powerful tools like Scapy and Impacket to understand and even test the defenses of digital systems. This first chapter is your launchpad, a friendly introduction to the core ideas of cybersecurity. Think of it as building a solid foundation before we start constructing our knowledge with code.

What Exactly is Cybersecurity?

Imagine our digital world – the internet, our computers, our phones – as a vast and intricate network of interconnected pathways. Cybersecurity, in essence, is the art and science of protecting this digital realm. It's about establishing defenses to keep the "good" data flowing safely and the "bad" stuff out.

At its core, cybersecurity aims to ensure three key principles, often referred to as the CIA Triad:

- Confidentiality: This is all about keeping secrets secret. Think of your passwords, personal emails, or sensitive business data. Cybersecurity measures ensure that only authorized individuals can access this information.

- Integrity: This principle focuses on maintaining the accuracy and trustworthiness of data. We need to be sure that our information hasn't been tampered with or corrupted, whether accidentally or maliciously.

- Availability: This means ensuring that authorized users can access the resources they need when they need them. Imagine trying to access your bank account online and the website is down due to a cyberattack – that's a loss of availability.

Beyond these core principles, cybersecurity also involves understanding the threats that exist and developing strategies to prevent, detect, and respond to them.

Why Cybersecurity Matters Now More Than Ever

You might be thinking, "Is all this security talk really that important?" The answer is a resounding yes! Our lives are increasingly intertwined with technology, making cybersecurity a critical aspect of our personal, professional, and even national well-being. Consider this:

- Digital Footprint: We leave digital footprints everywhere we go online – from social media to online shopping. All this data is a potential target.
- Interconnected World: The internet connects billions of devices and people. A vulnerability in one part of this network can potentially be exploited to reach others.
- Sophistication of Threats: Cyberattacks are no longer just the stuff of movies. They are real, sophisticated, and constantly evolving. From sneaky phishing emails to complex ransomware attacks that can lock down entire organizations, the threats are diverse and impactful.
- Real-World Consequences: A successful cyberattack can have serious consequences, including financial losses, identity theft, reputational damage, and even disruptions to critical infrastructure like power grids and healthcare systems.

- The Economic Impact: Cybercrime is a massive global industry, costing trillions of dollars annually. Protecting against these threats is not just about security; it's also about economic stability.

In this digital landscape, understanding how to secure systems and networks is no longer just for IT professionals. It's a crucial skill for anyone navigating the modern world, and especially for those looking to build a career in technology.

A Brief History of the Digital Battlefield

The need for cybersecurity emerged almost as soon as we started connecting computers. Here's a quick journey through its evolution:

- The Early Days (Pre-Internet Era): Security concerns in the early days of computing were primarily focused on physical access and preventing unauthorized use of mainframe computers. Basic password protection and access logs were among the initial measures.

- The Rise of Networking (Late 20th Century): As networks began to connect computers, new threats emerged. Early viruses and worms, like the Morris Worm in 1988, demonstrated the potential for malicious software to spread and cause disruption. This era saw the development of the first antivirus software and firewalls.

- The Internet Age (1990s - Early 2000s): The explosion of the internet brought about new attack vectors. Email-based viruses, website defacements, and early forms of denial-of-service attacks became more common. This period saw the rise of more sophisticated security tools and the beginnings of a dedicated cybersecurity industry.

- The Age of Sophistication (Mid-2000s - Present): Today, we face a highly complex threat landscape. Cybercriminals are organized, well-funded, and employ advanced techniques like social engineering, advanced persistent threats (APTs), and zero-day exploits. The proliferation of mobile devices, cloud computing, and the Internet of Things (IoT) has further expanded the attack surface.

This historical perspective highlights a crucial point: cybersecurity is a continuous arms race. As technology evolves, so do the threats, and our defenses must adapt accordingly. This is where your journey with Python, Scapy, and Impacket becomes so exciting. You'll be learning to understand the language of networks and how potential vulnerabilities can be exploited, empowering you to become a skilled defender in this ever-evolving digital battlefield.

So, welcome to the world of cybersecurity! This chapter has laid the groundwork, explaining what it is, why it's so important, and how it has evolved. Now, get ready to roll up your sleeves and dive into the practical aspects of mastering network security with Python in the chapters to come. The adventure is just beginning!

Chapter 2: Python Fundamentals for Cybersecurity

Welcome to the core of our toolkit! This chapter is all about equipping you with the Python knowledge you'll need to navigate the world of cybersecurity. We'll revisit fundamental Python concepts and highlight why they are particularly useful in our domain. Whether you're a Python beginner or have some experience, this chapter will provide a focused review and set you up for success in the more specialized topics ahead.

Revisiting Key Python Concepts for Security Pros

Python's versatility and readability make it a favorite among cybersecurity professionals. Let's refresh some core concepts that will be our workhorses:

- Variables and Data Types: At the heart of any programming language are variables, which act as containers for storing data. Python's dynamic typing allows us to assign different types of data to variables, such as:
  - Integers (int): Whole numbers (e.g., 10, -5). Useful for representing port numbers, packet lengths, etc.
  - Floats (float): Decimal numbers (e.g., 3.14, -0.01). Less common in basic networking but can be used for calculations.
  - Strings (str): Sequences of characters (e.g., "Hello", "192.168.1.1"). Essential for handling network protocols, commands, and output.
  - Booleans (bool): Representing truth values (True or False). Crucial for conditional logic in our scripts.

o Lists (list): Ordered collections of items (e.g., ["TCP", "UDP", "ICMP"]). Great for storing sequences of ports, IP addresses, or packet data.

o Tuples (tuple): Ordered, immutable collections (e.g., ("eth0", "192.168.1.100")). Useful for representing fixed sets of related data.

o Dictionaries (dict): Key-value pairs (e.g., {"port": 80, "protocol": "TCP"}). Excellent for organizing and accessing structured data, like packet headers.

- Operators: These are symbols that perform operations on variables and values. We'll frequently use:

o Arithmetic Operators: + (addition), - (subtraction), * (multiplication), / (division), // (floor division), % (modulo), ** (exponentiation). Useful for calculations involving packet sizes, time differences, etc.

- o Comparison Operators: == (equal to), != (not equal to), > (greater than), < (less than), >= (greater than or equal to), <= (less than or equal to). Essential for making decisions based on network conditions or packet content.

- o Logical Operators: and, or, not. Used to combine or negate boolean expressions, allowing for complex conditional logic in our scripts.

- o Assignment Operators: = (assign), +=, -=, *=, etc. (shorthand for combined operations).

- Control Flow: These structures allow us to control the order in which code is executed, making our scripts dynamic and responsive:

  - o Conditional Statements (if, elif, else): Allow us to execute different blocks of code based on whether certain conditions are true or false. This is fundamental for analyzing network traffic and making decisions based on packet characteristics.

- Loops (for, while): Enable us to repeat blocks of code multiple times. for loops are great for iterating over sequences (like lists of IP addresses), while while loops continue as long as a certain condition is true (useful for continuous network monitoring).

- break and continue: Statements that allow us to alter the flow of loops. break exits the loop prematurely, while continue skips the current iteration and moves to the next.

- Functions: These are reusable blocks of code that perform specific tasks. Defining functions helps organize our code, make it more readable, and avoid repetition. In cybersecurity, you might create functions to send specific types of packets, analyze network responses, or generate reports.

- Modules and Packages: Python's strength lies in its extensive library of modules and packages – collections of pre-written code that extend Python's functionality. For cybersecurity, we'll heavily rely on modules like socket for low-level networking, os for interacting with the operating system, and of course, the powerful libraries we're here to learn: Scapy and Impacket. Understanding how to import and use functions from these modules is crucial.

- File Handling: Cybersecurity tasks often involve reading from and writing to files – for example, reading lists of target IP addresses, storing captured network traffic, or logging results. Python's built-in file handling capabilities (open(), read(), write(), close(), and the with statement for automatic resource management) are essential.

- Error Handling (try, except): When dealing with network operations, things can sometimes go wrong (e.g., a host might be unreachable). Using try and except blocks allows us to gracefully handle errors and prevent our scripts from crashing.

Python Programming Language and Its Features

Beyond the basic concepts, Python boasts several features that make it particularly well-suited for cybersecurity:

- Readability and Simplicity: Python's syntax is designed to be clear and easy to understand, making it faster to write and maintain security scripts. This is crucial when dealing with complex network protocols and attack scenarios.

- Rapid Prototyping: Python's concise syntax and extensive libraries allow for quick development and testing of security tools and scripts. This agility is invaluable in a fast-paced threat landscape.

- Cross-Platform Compatibility: Python code can generally run on various operating systems (Windows, macOS, Linux) without significant modifications, making your security tools more versatile.

- Extensive Libraries: As mentioned earlier, Python's rich ecosystem of libraries provides ready-made solutions for a wide range of cybersecurity tasks, from network packet manipulation (Scapy) and protocol implementation (Impacket) to cryptography, web scraping, and forensic analysis.

- Community Support: Python has a large and active community, meaning you'll find plenty of resources, tutorials, and support forums to help you learn and troubleshoot.

Best Practices for Using Python in Cybersecurity

Writing effective and reliable Python code for cybersecurity requires adhering to certain best practices:

- Clarity and Readability: Write your code in a way that is easy for others (and your future self) to understand. Use meaningful variable names, add comments to explain complex logic, and follow consistent formatting conventions (e.g., PEP 8 style guide).

- Modularity and Reusability: Break down your code into functions and classes that perform specific tasks. This makes your code more organized, easier to test, and allows you to reuse components in different scripts.

- Error Handling: Implement robust error handling using try and except blocks to gracefully manage potential issues like network errors, file not found exceptions, or invalid user input. This prevents your tools from crashing unexpectedly.

- Input Validation: Always validate user input to prevent unexpected behavior or security vulnerabilities. For example, if you're expecting an IP address, ensure the input matches the correct format.

- Secure Coding Practices: Be mindful of potential security vulnerabilities in your own code. Avoid hardcoding sensitive information (like passwords), be cautious when using external libraries, and understand the implications of any system commands you execute.

- Documentation: Document your code with clear explanations of what it does, how to use it, and any important considerations. This is especially crucial if you plan to share your tools with others.

- Version Control: Use a version control system like Git to track changes to your code, collaborate effectively, and easily revert to previous versions if needed.

- Testing: Thoroughly test your scripts in a safe and controlled environment before using them on live systems. This helps identify and fix bugs and ensures your tools behave as expected.

By mastering these Python fundamentals and adhering to best practices, you'll build a strong foundation for leveraging the power of Scapy and Impacket in your cybersecurity endeavors. In the chapters that follow, we'll see these concepts in action as we delve into the exciting world of network manipulation and analysis. So, let's keep this knowledge fresh in our minds as we move forward!

Part 2: Scapy Fundamentals

Chapter 3: Introduction to Scapy

Welcome to the exciting world of network packet manipulation with Scapy! This chapter serves as your introduction to this incredible Python library. We'll explore its core functionalities, take a brief look at its history, and uncover the vast array of benefits and applications that make Scapy a cornerstone of cybersecurity work. Get ready to gain a new level of insight and control over network communications!

Unveiling Scapy: The Network Packet Swiss Army Knife

Scapy is more than just a Python library; it's an interactive packet manipulation tool and a powerful packet sniffer. It allows you to:

- Craft Network Packets: Imagine being able to build network packets from scratch, specifying every detail from the Ethernet frame to the application layer data. Scapy empowers you to create packets for virtually any protocol (TCP, UDP, ICMP, ARP, DNS, and many more).

- Send Packets: Once you've crafted your custom packets, Scapy allows you to send them out onto the network. This is invaluable for tasks like network discovery, vulnerability testing, and simulating various network conditions.

- Sniff Network Traffic: Scapy can also act as a network sniffer, capturing packets traversing your network. This allows you to observe real-time communication and analyze network behavior.

- Dissect Packets: When you capture or receive packets, Scapy provides a clear and structured way to dissect them, revealing the details of each protocol layer and the data being transmitted.

- Interact and Automate: Scapy's interactive console allows for real-time experimentation, while its Python library nature enables you to automate complex network tasks within your scripts.

Key features that make Scapy stand out include:

- Layered Approach: Scapy represents network protocols in a hierarchical layer structure, mirroring the OSI model or the TCP/IP model. This makes it intuitive to build and dissect packets by stacking protocol layers.
- Flexibility and Extensibility: Scapy supports a vast range of network protocols out of the box, and its design allows for easy extension to support new or custom protocols.
- Interactive Mode: The interactive Scapy shell provides a powerful environment for

experimenting with network packets in real time, making it an excellent tool for learning and quick analysis.

- Python Integration: Being a Python library, Scapy seamlessly integrates with other Python tools and libraries, allowing you to combine network manipulation with other functionalities like data analysis, reporting, and automation.

- Raw Socket Capabilities: Scapy operates at a low level, allowing you to bypass the operating system's network stack and have direct control over packet creation and transmission (this typically requires administrator/root privileges).

A Look Back: The Genesis and Evolution of Scapy

Scapy was created by Philippe Biondi, initially released in 2001. The motivation behind Scapy was to provide a more flexible and powerful alternative to existing packet manipulation tools, particularly those written in C. Here's a glimpse into its development:

- Early Inspiration: The need for a tool that could easily craft and dissect network packets for security testing and network analysis was a driving force. Existing tools often lacked the flexibility and ease of use that Python could offer.
- Python's Advantage: Choosing Python as the underlying language provided several benefits, including its readability, rapid development capabilities, and extensive standard library.
- Community Growth: Over the years, Scapy has garnered a strong and active community of users and developers who have contributed to its growth by adding support for new protocols, fixing bugs, and improving its features.

- Continued Development: Scapy continues to be actively maintained and updated, ensuring its compatibility with modern network technologies and addressing emerging security challenges. The project has seen contributions from numerous individuals, solidifying its position as a vital tool in the cybersecurity landscape.
- Scapy3k: An important evolution was the development of Scapy3k, a version of Scapy fully compatible with Python 3. This ensured the library's longevity and integration with the latest Python ecosystem.

The history of Scapy is a testament to the power of open-source collaboration and the need for flexible and adaptable tools in the ever-evolving field of network security.

Why Scapy is Your Ally: Benefits and Applications

Scapy offers a multitude of benefits and finds applications across various cybersecurity domains:

Benefits:

- Deep Network Understanding: By crafting and dissecting packets, you gain a profound understanding of how network protocols work at a fundamental level.
- Customization and Control: Scapy gives you granular control over every aspect of a network packet, allowing you to simulate specific network conditions and test edge cases.
- Rapid Prototyping of Security Tools: Scapy's ease of use and Python integration make it ideal for quickly prototyping custom security tools for tasks like network scanning, vulnerability assessment, and penetration testing.
- Effective Network Analysis: Scapy's sniffing and dissection capabilities are invaluable for

analyzing network traffic, identifying anomalies, and troubleshooting network issues.

- Educational Value: Scapy is an excellent tool for learning about network protocols and security concepts in a hands-on manner.

Applications:

- Network Discovery and Mapping: Sending probes (like ARP requests or ICMP echo requests) to identify active hosts and map network topology.
- Port Scanning: Crafting TCP SYN packets to determine open ports on target systems.
- Vulnerability Scanning: Creating and sending malformed or unexpected packets to test the robustness of network devices and applications.
- Penetration Testing: Simulating various attack scenarios, such as SYN floods, ARP

spoofing, and DNS poisoning, to assess the security posture of a network.

- Network Sniffing and Analysis: Capturing and analyzing network traffic to identify patterns, detect malicious activity, and troubleshoot network problems.

- Firewall and IDS Testing: Crafting packets designed to test the rules and effectiveness of firewalls and intrusion detection/prevention systems.

- Protocol Fuzzing: Generating a wide range of potentially malformed packets to identify vulnerabilities in network protocol implementations.

- Developing Custom Network Tools: Building specialized tools tailored to specific security needs or research purposes.

As you can see, Scapy is an incredibly versatile tool with a wide range of applications in cybersecurity. Mastering Scapy will significantly enhance your ability to understand, analyze, and interact with network traffic, making you a more effective security professional. In the following chapters, we'll start putting Scapy into action and exploring its practical uses. Get ready to unleash its power!

Chapter 4: Scapy Basics

Welcome to the practical heart of Scapy! In this chapter, we'll move beyond the introduction and delve into Scapy's core functionalities. You'll learn how to interact with Scapy, understand its layered structure, and perform essential tasks like crafting custom packets and exploring your network. Get ready to start building and dissecting packets like a pro!

Diving into Scapy's Core Components

Scapy's power comes from its intuitive way of representing network protocols and its interactive environment. Let's explore its key components:

- Layers: As we touched upon earlier, Scapy represents network protocols as layers. Each layer encapsulates specific information. For example, the Ethernet layer deals with MAC addresses, the IP layer handles IP addresses, and the TCP layer manages connections and data transfer. Scapy allows you to build packets by stacking these layers. Common layers you'll encounter include:

- Ethernet: The base layer for local network communication, dealing with MAC addresses (source and destination).

- ARP: Address Resolution Protocol, used to map IP addresses to MAC addresses within a local network.

- IP: Internet Protocol, responsible for routing packets across networks, containing source and destination IP addresses.

- TCP: Transmission Control Protocol, a connection-oriented protocol providing reliable data transfer.

○ UDP: User Datagram Protocol, a connectionless protocol offering faster but less reliable data transfer.

○ ICMP: Internet Control Message Protocol, used for sending control and error messages (like ping requests).

○ DNS: Domain Name System, used to translate domain names into IP addresses.

○ HTTP: Hypertext Transfer Protocol, the foundation of web communication.

• Fields: Each layer in Scapy is composed of fields, which are the specific pieces of information within that protocol. For example, the IP layer has fields like src (source IP address), dst (destination IP address), ttl (time-to-live), and proto (protocol). You can view and manipulate these fields when crafting or dissecting packets.

- Scapy Interactive Shell: This is where the magic often happens. By simply typing scapy in your terminal (after installing it), you launch an interactive Python environment with Scapy loaded. This shell allows you to:

  - Craft packets on the fly: Create and modify packets interactively.
  - Send and receive packets: Transmit your crafted packets and listen for responses.
  - Sniff network traffic: Capture packets passing through your network interface.
  - Inspect captured packets: Dissect and analyze the contents of captured packets.
  - Experiment and learn: The interactive nature makes it an excellent

environment for exploring network protocols.

- Packet Objects: When you craft, send, or receive a network packet in Scapy, it's represented as a Python object. These objects have attributes corresponding to the layers and fields of the packet. You can access and modify these attributes programmatically.
- Functions for Sending and Receiving: Scapy provides several key functions for interacting with the network:
  - send(): Sends packets at layer 3 (IP layer or above).
  - sendp(): Sends packets at layer 2 (Ethernet layer or below), allowing for more control over the link layer.
  - sr(): Sends packets and captures the responses at layer 3. It returns two lists: sent packets and received packets.

- srp(): Sends packets and captures the responses at layer 2.
- sniff(): Captures network packets based on specified filters.

Using Scapy for Packet Manipulation and Network Exploration

Let's walk through some basic examples to illustrate how to use Scapy for packet manipulation and network exploration:

- Crafting a Simple Ping Request (ICMP Echo Request):
- Python

```python
from scapy.all import IP, ICMP, send

# Create an IP layer
ip_layer = IP(dst="192.168.1.1")

# Create an ICMP layer (echo request is the default)
```

```
icmp_layer = ICMP()

# Combine the layers to form the packet
packet = ip_layer / icmp_layer

# Send the packet
send(packet)
```

-
- In this example, we import the necessary layers, create instances of IP and ICMP, specify the destination IP address in the IP layer, and then combine them using the / operator. Finally, we use the send() function to transmit the crafted ICMP echo request.
- Sending and Receiving a Ping and Analyzing the Response:
- Python

```
from scapy.all import IP, ICMP, sr1

# Craft the ping request
```

```
packet = IP(dst="google.com") / ICMP()

# Send the packet and capture the first response
response = sr1(packet, timeout=1, verbose=0)

# Check if a response was received
if response:
    print("Received a response:")
    response.show()
else:
    print("No response received.")
```

-
  - Here, we use sr1() (send and receive one packet) to send an ICMP echo request to Google's IP address and wait for a response. The verbose=0 argument suppresses the display of sent packets. If a response is received, we use the .show() method to display its details.
- Exploring Network Hosts with ARP:
- Python

```python
from scapy.all import Ether, ARP, srp

# Define the target IP range (replace with your
network)
ip_range = "192.168.1.1/24"

# Create an ARP request packet
arp_request   =   Ether(dst="ff:ff:ff:ff:ff:ff")   /
ARP(pdst=ip_range)

# Send the packet and capture the responses
answered,    unanswered    =    srp(arp_request,
timeout=2, verbose=0)

print("Available devices on the network:")
for sent, received in answered:
        print(f"IP:  {received.psrc}  -  MAC:
{received.hwsrc}")
```

-
- This example uses ARP (Address Resolution
  Protocol) to discover active hosts on a local

network. We create an Ethernet frame with the broadcast MAC address and an ARP request asking for the MAC address associated with each IP in the specified range. srp() at layer 2 is used to send and receive the ARP replies.

- **Sniffing Network Traffic:**
- Python

```python
from scapy.all import sniff

def packet_callback(packet):
  print(packet.summary())

# Sniff for 10 packets
sniff(count=10, prn=packet_callback)

# Sniff for traffic on a specific port (e.g., HTTP port 80)
# sniff(filter="tcp port 80", prn=packet_callback)
```
  -

- The sniff() function allows you to capture network traffic. The count parameter specifies the number of packets to capture, and the prn parameter takes a function that will be called for each captured packet. The filter parameter allows you to specify Berkeley Packet Filter (BPF) syntax to capture only specific types of traffic.

Best Practices for Using Scapy in Cybersecurity

Using Scapy effectively and responsibly is crucial. Here are some best practices to keep in mind:

- Understand the Legal and Ethical Implications: Network scanning and packet manipulation can have legal and ethical ramifications. Always ensure you have explicit permission before testing or interacting with networks that you own or have been authorized to assess.

- Use Scapy Responsibly: Avoid using Scapy for malicious purposes. Its power should be used for learning, security testing with permission, and network analysis.
- Start Small and Understand Each Step: When crafting packets, build them layer by layer and verify each step. Use packet.show() to inspect the structure and contents of your packets.
- Be Mindful of Network Impact: Sending too many packets too quickly can overwhelm network devices and potentially disrupt services. Use appropriate timeouts and rate limiting when necessary.
- Filter Your Sniffing: When capturing network traffic, use filters to narrow down the packets you're interested in. This will make analysis much more manageable and reduce the load on your system.
- Understand Protocol Specifications: To effectively craft and analyze packets, it's

essential to have a good understanding of the underlying network protocols you're working with (e.g., TCP/IP, HTTP, DNS).

- Practice in Isolated Environments: When experimenting with packet crafting and sending, it's highly recommended to do so in a controlled and isolated lab environment to avoid unintended consequences on live networks.

- Document Your Code: If you're writing scripts using Scapy, add comments to explain what your code is doing. This will help you and others understand and maintain your scripts.

- Keep Scapy Updated: Regularly update Scapy to benefit from the latest features, bug fixes, and security enhancements.

By understanding Scapy's core components and following these best practices, you're well on your way to harnessing its power for network exploration and cybersecurity tasks.

In the subsequent chapters, we'll build upon these basics and explore more advanced techniques and applications of Scapy. Let the packet manipulation begin!

Chapter 5: Advanced Scapy Topics

Welcome to the realm of advanced Scapy usage! This chapter will take your skills to the next level. We'll explore the intricate art of crafting and injecting custom network packets, delve into how Scapy becomes a powerful ally in network security assessments and penetration testing engagements, and provide you with essential techniques for debugging your Scapy scripts. Prepare to become a true Scapy ninja!

Mastering Advanced Packet Crafting and Injection

Beyond the basic layer stacking, Scapy offers powerful features for creating highly customized and even malformed packets. This level of control is crucial for advanced network analysis and security testing.

- Customizing Layer Fields: You're not limited to the default values of packet fields. Scapy allows you to set any field to any arbitrary value. This is essential for simulating specific network conditions or crafting packets for particular attack scenarios. For example:
- Python

```
from scapy.all import IP, TCP, send

# Craft a TCP SYN packet with a specific source
port and flags
syn_packet                                    =
IP(dst="192.168.1.100")/TCP(sport=12345,
dport=80, flags="S")
send(syn_packet, verbose=0)
```

```
# Craft an IP packet with a custom TTL
(Time-To-Live)
custom_ttl_packet    =    IP(dst="example.com",
ttl=64)/ICMP()
send(custom_ttl_packet, verbose=0)
```

-
  - Here, we demonstrate setting specific source and destination ports, TCP flags, and the IP TTL field.
  - Adding Raw Payloads: Scapy allows you to add raw data payloads to your packets. This is useful for testing how systems handle unexpected data or for injecting specific attack payloads.
  - Python

```
from scapy.all import IP, TCP, Raw, send

# Craft a TCP packet with a custom data payload
payload = b"This is some custom data!"
```

```python
data_packet                                    =
IP(dst="192.168.1.100")/TCP(dport=80)/Raw(loa
d=payload)
send(data_packet, verbose=0)
```

-
  - The Raw layer allows you to inject arbitrary byte strings as the packet's data.
  - Fragmenting IP Packets: In some cases, you might need to send IP packets that are larger than the network's Maximum Transmission Unit (MTU). Scapy can automatically fragment these packets for you.
  - Python

```python
from scapy.all import IP, TCP, Raw, send

# Create a large payload
large_payload = b"A" * 2000

# Craft a TCP packet with the large payload (Scapy
will handle fragmentation)
```

```
large_packet                              =
IP(dst="192.168.1.100")/TCP(dport=80)/Raw(loa
d=large_payload)
send(large_packet, verbose=0)
```

-
- Scapy will automatically add the necessary IP fragmentation headers.
- Crafting Packets with Multiple Layers: You can build complex packets by stacking various protocol layers in a specific order to simulate different network scenarios.
- Python

```
from scapy.all import Ether, IP, UDP, DNS, DNSQR, sendp

# Craft a DNS query packet at layer 2
ether_layer = Ether(dst="ff:ff:ff:ff:ff:ff")
ip_layer = IP(dst="8.8.8.8")
udp_layer = UDP(dport=53)
```

```
dns_query                =                DNS(rd=1,
qd=DNSQR(qname="example.com"))
```
packet = ether_layer/ip_layer/udp_layer/dns_query
sendp(packet, iface="eth0", verbose=0) # Use sendp
for layer 2 sending

-
- Remember to use sendp() when you're including layer 2 information (like the Ethernet frame) and need more control over the link layer. Specify the network interface using the iface parameter.
- Packet Injection Techniques: Scapy's send() and sendp() functions are used for packet injection. Understanding the difference is crucial:
  - send() operates at layer 3 (IP layer and above). The operating system's network stack handles the lower-level details like MAC address resolution.
  - sendp() operates at layer 2 (Ethernet layer and below), giving you direct

control over the entire frame. This often requires root/administrator privileges and specifying the network interface.

Scapy for Network Security and Penetration Testing

Scapy becomes an invaluable tool when it comes to assessing the security of networks and systems. Here are some key applications in this domain:

- Network Scanning and Enumeration:
    - Port Scanning: Crafting various TCP and UDP probes (SYN, ACK, FIN, NULL, XMAS scans) to identify open ports and infer the state of target services.
    - Host Discovery: Using ARP requests or ICMP echo requests to identify active hosts on a network.

- OS Fingerprinting: Sending specially crafted TCP packets and analyzing the responses to try and identify the operating system of a target host.

- Vulnerability Assessment:
  - Firewall Testing: Crafting packets designed to test firewall rules and identify potential bypasses.
  - IDS/IPS Evasion: Creating fragmented or malformed packets to see if intrusion detection/prevention systems can correctly identify and block them.
  - Protocol-Specific Vulnerability Testing: Crafting packets that exploit known vulnerabilities in specific network protocols or services.

- Penetration Testing and Attack Simulation:
  - Denial of Service (DoS) Attacks: Generating a large volume of traffic (e.g., SYN floods, UDP floods) to

overwhelm target systems. (Use with extreme caution and only with explicit permission!)

- o Man-in-the-Middle (MITM) Attacks: Crafting and injecting ARP packets to poison the ARP cache of hosts on a local network, potentially intercepting traffic.
- o DNS Spoofing: Crafting malicious DNS responses to redirect traffic to attacker-controlled systems.
- o DHCP Attacks: Sending rogue DHCP messages to disrupt network configuration.
- Wireless Security Testing: Scapy can be used to craft and inject wireless frames for tasks like:
  - o Probe Request/Response Analysis: Observing wireless client and access point behavior.

- Deauthentication Attacks: Forcibly disconnecting wireless clients from access points (for testing purposes only!).
- WEP/WPA/WPA2 Packet Analysis: Capturing and analyzing wireless traffic for security assessments.

Important Ethical Consideration: Remember that using these techniques against systems without explicit permission is illegal and unethical. Always ensure you have proper authorization before conducting any security testing.

Troubleshooting and Debugging Techniques for Scapy

Like any powerful tool, you might encounter issues when using Scapy. Here are some common problems and debugging techniques:

- Permission Errors: Sending raw packets often requires root or administrator privileges. Ensure you are running your Scapy scripts with the necessary permissions.

- Interface Issues: Make sure you have the correct network interface specified when using functions like sendp() or sniff(). You can list available interfaces using scapy.all.get_if_list().
- Packet Not Sent/Received:
    - Firewall Interference: Local firewalls on your testing machine or the target system might be blocking the packets. Temporarily disable firewalls for testing (with caution).
    - Incorrect Layering or Fields: Double-check that you have constructed your packets correctly, with the layers in the right order and the fields set to the intended values. Use packet.show() to inspect your crafted packets.

- Routing Issues: Ensure that your system has a route to the target network.
- Network Connectivity: Verify basic network connectivity to the target host using tools like ping.
- Scapy Not Installed or Import Errors: Ensure that Scapy is correctly installed in your Python environment. If you get import errors, try reinstalling Scapy using pip install scapy.
- Unexpected Sniffing Results:
  - Incorrect Filters: Double-check your sniff() filters to ensure they are capturing the traffic you're interested in. Refer to Berkeley Packet Filter (BPF) syntax documentation.
  - Promiscuous Mode: For capturing all traffic on a network segment (not just traffic destined for or originating from your machine), your network

interface needs to be in promiscuous mode. Scapy usually handles this automatically, but issues can sometimes arise.

- Using verbose: Many Scapy functions have a verbose parameter (default is often 1). Setting it to 2 or higher can provide more detailed output about what Scapy is doing, which can be helpful for debugging. Setting it to 0 suppresses most output.

- Interactive Shell for Testing: Use the interactive Scapy shell to test small snippets of code and experiment with packet crafting before incorporating them into larger scripts. This can help isolate issues.

- Consulting Documentation and Community: The official Scapy documentation and online communities (forums, Stack Overflow) are valuable resources for troubleshooting and finding solutions to common problems.

By mastering these advanced Scapy techniques and honing your troubleshooting skills, you'll be well-equipped to tackle complex network security challenges and leverage the full power of this remarkable library. The journey into advanced packet manipulation and security testing is an exciting one – let's continue to explore!

Part 3: Impacket Fundamentals

Chapter 6: Introduction to Impacket

Welcome to the world of Impacket! In this chapter, we'll introduce you to this fantastic Python library that specializes in network protocols, with a strong emphasis on Microsoft Windows network protocols. We'll explore its capabilities, delve into its history, and uncover the numerous benefits and applications that make Impacket an essential tool for penetration testers, security analysts, and anyone working with Windows-based networks. Get ready to gain a new level of interaction with network services!

Unveiling Impacket: Your Python Toolkit for Network Protocols

Impacket is a collection of Python classes for working with network protocols. Unlike Scapy, which provides low-level packet crafting and sniffing capabilities, Impacket focuses on the implementation and parsing of higher-level protocols. It allows you to programmatically interact with network services and protocols as if you were using native tools.

Key features of Impacket include:

- Protocol Implementation: Impacket provides implementations for a wide range of network protocols, including:
  - Ethernet, IP, TCP, UDP: Foundational network protocols.
  - SMB (Server Message Block): The protocol used for file sharing, printing, and inter-process communication in Windows networks.
  - NetBIOS: Network Basic Input/Output System, an older

naming and session layer protocol used in Windows environments.

- MSRPC (Microsoft Remote Procedure Call): A protocol that allows one program to request a service from another program on a network. Many critical Windows services rely on MSRPC.
- Kerberos: The primary authentication protocol used in Windows domains.
- LDAP (Lightweight Directory Access Protocol): Used for accessing and managing directory information, often used with Active Directory.
- NTLM (NT LAN Manager): An older authentication protocol used in Windows.
- DNS (Domain Name System): For resolving domain names to IP addresses.

- HTTP (Hypertext Transfer Protocol): The foundation of web communication.
- Object-Oriented Approach: Impacket represents protocol structures as Python objects, making it easy to create, parse, and manipulate protocol data.
- High-Level Abstractions: Impacket provides higher-level functions and classes that simplify interaction with network services. For example, you can easily perform SMB file operations, execute remote commands via MSRPC, or interact with LDAP directories without needing to manually construct the underlying protocol messages.
- Focus on Windows Protocols: While it supports some general network protocols, Impacket's strength lies in its comprehensive support for protocols commonly found in Windows environments, making it

invaluable for assessing the security of these systems.

- No External Dependencies (Mostly): Impacket is primarily written in pure Python and has minimal external dependencies, making it relatively easy to install and deploy.

A Look Back: The Genesis and Evolution of Impacket

Impacket was initially developed by Alberto Solino. The primary goal was to create a Python library that would simplify the process of working with network protocols, especially those prevalent in Windows environments, for security auditing and penetration testing purposes.

- Addressing the Need: Security professionals often needed to interact with Windows systems using their native protocols. Existing tools sometimes lacked the flexibility and programmatic access that a Python library could offer.

- Focus on SMB and MSRPC: Early development heavily focused on implementing SMB and MSRPC, which are fundamental to many Windows-based attacks and security assessments.

- Community Contributions: Over time, Impacket has benefited from contributions from a growing community of security researchers and developers who have added support for more protocols, improved existing implementations, and fixed bugs.

- Integration with Other Tools: Impacket has become a foundational library for many other security tools and frameworks, highlighting its importance in the cybersecurity ecosystem.

- Continued Development: The Impacket project continues to be actively maintained, with new features and protocol support being added to address the evolving threat landscape.

The development of Impacket has significantly empowered security professionals by providing a programmatic way to interact with and analyze Windows network protocols, leading to more effective security assessments and the development of sophisticated attack and defense tools.

Why Impacket is Your Ally: Benefits and Applications

Impacket offers a unique set of benefits and finds applications in various cybersecurity tasks, particularly those involving Windows environments:

Benefits:

- High-Level Protocol Interaction: Simplifies interaction with network services by providing abstractions over low-level packet manipulation.

- Focus on Windows Environments: Provides comprehensive support for key Windows network protocols like SMB, MSRPC, Kerberos, and NTLM.
- Programmatic Control: Allows for automation of tasks that would otherwise require manual interaction with various command-line tools.
- Extensibility: Its object-oriented design makes it relatively easy to extend and customize for specific needs.
- Integration with Python Ecosystem: Seamlessly integrates with other Python libraries for tasks like data analysis, reporting, and automation.
- Understanding Protocol Internals: By working with Impacket, you gain a deeper understanding of how these network protocols function.

Applications:

- Authentication Attacks: Implementing and testing various authentication attacks against Windows systems, such as password spraying, Kerberos exploitation (e.g., AS-REP Roasting, Kerberoasting), and NTLM relay attacks.
- Remote Command Execution: Leveraging protocols like SMB and MSRPC to execute commands on remote Windows systems.
- File Sharing and Manipulation: Programmatically interacting with SMB shares to upload, download, and manipulate files.
- Active Directory Interaction: Using LDAP to query and manipulate objects within Active Directory.
- Credential Dumping: Implementing methods to extract credentials from Windows systems using protocols like MSRPC.

- Lateral Movement: Utilizing protocols like SMB and MSRPC to move laterally between compromised systems within a network.
- Vulnerability Exploitation: Developing exploits that leverage vulnerabilities in Windows network services.
- Security Auditing: Automating security checks and assessments of Windows network configurations and services.
- Building Custom Security Tools: Creating specialized tools for tasks like network reconnaissance, vulnerability scanning, and post-exploitation.

In essence, Impacket provides the building blocks for programmatically interacting with Windows network services, making it an indispensable tool for anyone involved in assessing or securing Windows-based environments.

In the following chapters, we'll start exploring practical examples of how to use Impacket to perform various security-related tasks. Get ready to unlock the power of Windows network protocol interaction with Python!

Chapter 7: Impacket Basics

Welcome to the practical introduction to Impacket! In this chapter, we'll delve into the core functionalities of this powerful Python library. You'll learn about its key components, how to use it to dissect and interact with network protocols like SMB and MSRPC, and the best practices to follow when leveraging Impacket for security-related tasks. Get ready to start programmatically engaging with network services!

Exploring Impacket's Core Components

Impacket provides a structured and object-oriented way to work with network protocols. Let's explore its key components:

- Protocol Implementations: At the heart of Impacket are its implementations of various network protocols. These implementations consist of Python classes that define the structure and fields of protocol messages. For instance, you'll find classes for SMB, MSRPC, Kerberos, and many others. These classes allow you to:

- Create Protocol Objects: Instantiate objects representing specific protocol messages (e.g., an SMB session setup request, an MSRPC bind request).

- Set and Retrieve Fields: Access and manipulate the individual fields within these protocol messages.

- Build and Parse Messages: Convert the Python objects into their raw byte representations for sending over the network and vice versa.

- Connection Objects: Impacket provides classes for establishing network connections using specific protocols. For example:

- o SMBConnection: For establishing SMB connections to remote servers.
- o DCERPCStringBinding: For defining the string binding used to connect to MSRPC services.
- o LDAP: For establishing LDAP connections to directory servers. These connection objects handle the underlying socket communication and protocol-specific handshakes.
- Client Classes: Impacket often provides higher-level client classes that encapsulate common interactions with network services. These clients build upon the protocol implementations and connection objects to offer a more user-friendly interface for performing specific tasks. Examples include:
  - o SMBClient: For interacting with SMB shares (listing files, uploading, downloading).

- MSRPCClientProtocol: A base class for interacting with various MSRPC services, with specialized implementations for specific services (e.g., DRSClientProtocol for Directory Replication Service).
- LDAPClient: For performing LDAP operations (searching, adding, modifying entries).
- Examples and Utilities: Impacket comes with a wealth of example scripts and command-line utilities that demonstrate its capabilities. These can serve as excellent starting points for learning how to use the library and for performing common security tasks. You'll find tools for password spraying, remote command execution, and more.

Using Impacket for Network Protocol Analysis and Exploitation

Let's look at some basic examples to illustrate how to use Impacket for interacting with network protocols:

- Basic SMB Connection and Listing Shares:
- Python

```python
from impacket import smb

try:
    conn = smb.SMB('192.168.1.100', '\\\\192.168.1.100')
    shares = conn.listShares()
    print("Shares on \\\\192.168.1.100:")
    for share in shares:
        print(f" - {share['shi1_netname']}")
    conn.close()
except Exception as e:
    print(f"Error connecting to SMB: {e}")
```

-

- This example demonstrates establishing an SMB connection to a remote host and listing the available shares.
- Interacting with an MSRPC Service (Getting Server Time):
- Python

```python
from impacket.dcerpc.v5 import rprn
from impacket.dcerpc.v5.transport import DCERPCTransportFactory

try:
    stringBinding = r"ncacn_np:\\192.168.1.100[\PIPE\wkssvc]"
    rpctransport = DCERPCTransportFactory(stringBinding)
    dce = rpctransport.get_dce_rpc()
    dce.connect()
    resp = rprn.hNetrServerGetInfo(dce, 100)
    print(f"Server Time: {resp['ServerInfo100']['sv100_time']}")
```

```python
        dce.disconnect()
except Exception as e:
    print(f"Error interacting with MSRPC: {e}")
```

-
- This example shows how to connect to the wkssvc (Workstation Service) MSRPC interface on a remote host and retrieve the server's current time.
- Performing an LDAP Query (Requires Authentication):
- Python

```python
from impacket import ldap

try:
    ldap_con = ldap.LDAP('ldap://192.168.1.10')
    ldap_con.login('username', 'password') # Replace
with valid credentials

        attributes = ['sAMAccountName',
'displayName']
```

```python
        results          =
ldap_con.search(baseDN='DC=example,DC=com'
,
            scope=ldap.SCOPE_SUBTREE,

searchFilter='(objectCategory=person)',
                attributes=attributes)

    print("Users in the domain:")
    for dn, entry in results.items():
            if isinstance(entry, dict) and
'sAMAccountName' in entry:
                print(f"    - Username:
{entry['sAMAccountName'][0].decode()}, Display
Name: {entry['displayName'][0].decode()}")

    ldap_con.unbind()
except Exception as e:
    print(f"Error interacting with LDAP: {e}")
    ●
```

- This example demonstrates how to connect to an LDAP server, authenticate, and perform a search for user objects, retrieving their username and display name. Remember to replace 'username' and 'password' with valid credentials and adjust the baseDN to your target domain.

These are just basic examples to illustrate the fundamental way you interact with network protocols using Impacket. The library provides much more extensive capabilities for each protocol.

Best Practices for Using Impacket in Cybersecurity

Using Impacket effectively and responsibly is crucial for ethical and successful security engagements. Here are some best practices to keep in mind:

- Understand the Protocols: Before using Impacket to interact with a specific protocol, ensure you have a solid understanding of how that protocol works. This will help you craft meaningful requests and interpret the responses correctly.

- Use Credentials Responsibly: When performing actions that require authentication, always use credentials that you have explicit permission to use. Avoid attempting to guess or brute-force passwords without authorization.

- Be Mindful of Network Impact: Some Impacket tools and techniques can generate significant network traffic or interact with critical services. Use them judiciously and be aware of the potential impact on the target systems.

- Start with Reconnaissance: Before attempting any exploitation, use Impacket to gather information about the target environment. This can help you identify potential vulnerabilities and tailor your approach.

- Leverage Existing Examples and Utilities: Impacket's provided examples and utilities can be a great starting point for your tasks. Understand how they work and modify them to suit your specific needs.

- Handle Exceptions Gracefully: Network interactions can be prone to errors. Use `try...except` blocks to handle potential exceptions and prevent your scripts from crashing.

- Log Your Activities: Keep a record of the actions you perform using Impacket, especially during security assessments. This is important for reporting and analysis.

- Respect Boundaries: Always operate within the scope of your authorization and avoid actions that could cause harm or disruption to the target systems.

- Keep Impacket Updated: Regularly update Impacket to benefit from the latest features, bug fixes, and security enhancements.

By understanding Impacket's core components and adhering to these best practices, you'll be well-equipped to leverage its power for network protocol analysis and ethical security testing, particularly within Windows environments. In the chapters that follow, we'll delve into more specific and advanced use cases of Impacket. Let's continue our journey into the world of Windows network security!

Chapter 8: Advanced Impacket Topics

Welcome to the advanced realm of Impacket! In this chapter, we'll go beyond the basics and explore the more intricate features of this powerful library. We'll dissect the complexities of SMB and MSRPC protocol analysis, uncover how Impacket can be used for advanced network security assessments and penetration testing scenarios, and provide you with the essential techniques for troubleshooting and debugging your Impacket endeavors. Prepare to become a true Impacket master!

Deep Dive into SMB and MSRPC Protocol Analysis with Impacket

Impacket's strength lies in its robust implementations of protocols like SMB and MSRPC. Understanding how to leverage these implementations for in-depth analysis is crucial for advanced security work.

- Advanced SMB Interaction:
  - File Operations: Beyond listing shares, Impacket allows for granular control over file operations, including creating, reading, writing, and deleting files and directories. This can be invaluable for assessing file share permissions and identifying potential vulnerabilities.
  - Named Pipes: SMB named pipes are a mechanism for inter-process communication. Impacket enables you to interact with named pipes, which can be used to access various services and potentially exploit vulnerabilities.
  - Authentication Mechanisms: Impacket provides detailed control over SMB authentication, allowing

you to test different authentication methods and identify weaknesses. You can specify NTLM hashes, Kerberos tickets, and more.

- Protocol Negotiation: Understanding how SMB clients and servers negotiate protocol versions and capabilities is essential for identifying potential downgrade attacks or compatibility issues. Impacket allows you to observe and influence this negotiation process.

- SMB Packet Analysis: Impacket's object-oriented structure allows you to dissect and analyze the individual components of SMB packets, providing insights into the communication flow and potential anomalies.

- Advanced MSRPC Interaction:
  - Understanding DCE/RPC String Bindings: Impacket helps you

construct and manipulate DCE/RPC string bindings, which specify how to connect to a particular MSRPC service on a remote host. Understanding these bindings is key to targeting specific services.

- Working with Different MSRPC Interfaces: MSRPC encompasses a vast array of interfaces, each providing access to different functionalities. Impacket provides implementations for many common and security-relevant interfaces (e.g., svcctl for service control, samr for Security Account Manager, lsarpc for Local Security Authority).
- Performing Specific MSRPC Operations: For each interface, Impacket provides functions corresponding to the various Remote Procedure Calls (RPCs) that can be

invoked. Understanding the parameters and responses of these RPCs is crucial for interacting with the services effectively.

- Authentication and Authorization in MSRPC: MSRPC supports various authentication levels. Impacket allows you to specify authentication credentials and levels when connecting to services, enabling you to test access controls.

- Analyzing MSRPC Traffic: Impacket's structure allows you to examine the requests and responses exchanged during MSRPC communication, which can be vital for understanding service behavior and identifying potential vulnerabilities.

Leveraging Impacket for Advanced Network Security and Penetration Testing

Building upon the advanced protocol analysis capabilities, Impacket becomes a powerful tool for sophisticated security testing:

- Advanced Authentication Attacks:
  - Pass-the-Hash: Impacket enables you to leverage NTLM hashes obtained from compromised systems to authenticate to other systems without needing the plaintext password.
  - Pass-the-Ticket: Impacket allows you to use Kerberos ticket-granting tickets (TGTs) and service tickets to authenticate to resources, bypassing the need for password-based authentication.
  - Kerberoasting and AS-REP Roasting: Impacket provides tools to exploit weaknesses in Kerberos

configurations to obtain password hashes.

- o NTLM Relay Attacks: Impacket can be used to set up NTLM relay servers to intercept and relay authentication attempts to other services.
- Remote Code Execution:
    - o Exploiting MSRPC Vulnerabilities: Impacket can be used to develop and execute exploits targeting vulnerabilities in various MSRPC services.
    - o Leveraging WMI (Windows Management Instrumentation): Impacket provides ways to interact with WMI, which can sometimes be used to execute commands on remote systems.
    - o Service Control Manipulation: Using the svcctl MSRPC interface, Impacket can be used to create, start,

stop, and delete services on remote systems (with appropriate privileges).

- Lateral Movement Techniques:
  - SMB Session Hijacking: Impacket can be used to attempt to hijack existing SMB sessions.
  - Psexec-like Functionality: Impacket implements its own versions of tools like Psexec, allowing for remote command execution and file transfer over SMB and MSRPC.
  - DCOM Exploitation: Impacket provides tools to interact with Distributed Component Object Model (DCOM), which can sometimes be leveraged for lateral movement.
- Active Directory Security Assessment:
  - LDAP Manipulation: Impacket allows for advanced LDAP queries and modifications, enabling you to

gather detailed information about Active Directory objects and potentially identify misconfigurations.

- o Group Policy Analysis: While not a direct Impacket feature, its LDAP capabilities can be used to retrieve and analyze Group Policy Objects (GPOs).
- o Domain Trust Analysis: Impacket can be used to query domain trust relationships.

Ethical Considerations Revisited: As with advanced Scapy techniques, remember that using these advanced Impacket capabilities requires explicit permission and should only be performed in authorized testing environments. Unauthorized use is illegal and unethical.

Advanced Troubleshooting and Debugging Techniques for Impacket

When working with Impacket's advanced features, you might encounter more complex issues. Here are some advanced troubleshooting and debugging techniques:

- Detailed Protocol Analysis: Use network analysis tools like Wireshark in conjunction with your Impacket scripts to examine the raw network traffic being exchanged. This can help you pinpoint issues in protocol negotiation, message formatting, or authentication sequences.

- Examining Impacket Source Code: Since Impacket is open source, don't hesitate to dive into the source code of the relevant protocol implementations and client classes. This can provide valuable insights into how the library works and help you identify potential issues in your usage.

- Debugging Authentication Issues: Authentication problems can be complex. Pay close attention to error messages returned by Impacket and the target system. Use tools like Kerberos debugging tools (klist, kdestroy) if you suspect Kerberos-related issues.

- Tracing MSRPC Calls: When working with MSRPC, try to trace the sequence of RPC calls being made and examine the parameters and return values. This can help you understand if the communication is proceeding as expected.

- Isolating the Problem: If you're encountering an issue, try to isolate the specific part of your code or the specific protocol interaction that is causing the problem. Simplify your script to focus on the problematic area.

- Leveraging Logging: Impacket might provide some internal logging capabilities.

Explore the documentation to see if you can enable more verbose logging to understand the library's internal operations.

- Testing Against Known Good Configurations: If you're unsure if your Impacket code is correct, try testing it against a known good and well-configured system to see if it works as expected.

- Utilizing Online Resources and Communities: The Impacket GitHub repository, online forums, and security communities are valuable resources for finding solutions to complex issues and learning from the experiences of others.

By mastering these advanced Impacket topics and honing your debugging skills, you'll be well-equipped to tackle sophisticated network security challenges in Windows environments. The ability to analyze and interact with protocols like SMB and MSRPC at this level opens up a wide range of possibilities for security assessments and penetration testing. Keep exploring and experimenting responsibly!

Part 4: Network Security and Penetration Testing

Chapter 9: Network Security Fundamentals

Welcome to the bedrock of our practical explorations! In this chapter, we shift our focus to the underlying principles that govern secure network communication. We'll explore the core concepts and threats in network security, understand why it's a cornerstone of overall cybersecurity, and lay out the essential best practices for designing, implementing, and maintaining secure network infrastructures. This knowledge will provide the vital context for the hands-on work we've been doing with Scapy and Impacket.

Understanding Core Network Security Concepts and Threats

Network security encompasses a wide range of strategies and technologies aimed at protecting the confidentiality, integrity, and availability of network resources and data. Let's delve into some of the fundamental concepts:

- Confidentiality in Networks: Ensuring that sensitive network traffic and data are only accessible to authorized individuals or systems. This is often achieved through encryption, access controls, and secure protocols.
- Integrity in Networks: Maintaining the accuracy and reliability of network data. This involves preventing unauthorized modification, deletion, or corruption of data in transit and at rest. Techniques include hashing, digital signatures, and access controls.
- Availability in Networks: Ensuring that network resources and services are accessible to authorized users when they need them.

This involves implementing measures to prevent and mitigate disruptions like denial-of-service (DoS) attacks and hardware failures.

- Access Control: Limiting who or what can access network resources. This includes authentication (verifying identity) and authorization (granting permissions). Common mechanisms include passwords, multi-factor authentication, and role-based access control (RBAC).

- Perimeter Security: Establishing a boundary around the network to control incoming and outgoing traffic. Firewalls, intrusion detection/prevention systems (IDS/IPS), and web proxies are key components of perimeter security.

- Network Segmentation: Dividing the network into smaller, isolated segments to limit the impact of a security breach. If one segment is compromised, the attacker's ability to move laterally to other parts of the network is restricted.

- Endpoint Security: Protecting individual devices (laptops, desktops, servers, mobile devices) that connect to the network. This includes antivirus software, endpoint detection and response (EDR) solutions, and host-based firewalls.

- Wireless Security: Securing wireless networks using protocols like WPA3, implementing strong passwords, and controlling access.

- VPNs (Virtual Private Networks): Creating secure, encrypted tunnels over public networks to ensure the confidentiality and integrity of data transmitted between remote users or networks.

- Network Monitoring and Analysis: Continuously monitoring network traffic for suspicious activity, performance issues, and security incidents. Tools like network sniffers (which Scapy can emulate), log analysis systems, and security information and event management (SIEM) platforms are crucial here.

Understanding these concepts is essential for appreciating the purpose and impact of the tools and techniques we've explored with Scapy and Impacket. They allow us to test the effectiveness of these security controls and identify potential weaknesses.

Now, let's consider the common threats that network security aims to defend against:

- Malware: Malicious software (viruses, worms, Trojans, ransomware, spyware) that can infiltrate networks and cause damage, steal data, or disrupt operations.
- Phishing and Social Engineering: Deceptive tactics used to trick users into revealing sensitive information or granting unauthorized access.

- Denial-of-Service (DoS) and Distributed Denial-of-Service (DDoS) Attacks: Overwhelming network resources with traffic to make them unavailable to legitimate users.

- Man-in-the-Middle (MITM) Attacks: Intercepting communication between two parties to eavesdrop or manipulate data.

- Eavesdropping and Packet Sniffing: Capturing network traffic to gain unauthorized access to sensitive information. (This is where tools like Scapy can be used for both legitimate analysis and malicious purposes).

- Spoofing Attacks: Falsifying source IP addresses, MAC addresses, email addresses, or other identifiers to impersonate legitimate entities. (Scapy is excellent for crafting such spoofed packets for testing).

- Insider Threats: Security risks posed by individuals with legitimate access to network resources who misuse their privileges.

- Exploitation of Vulnerabilities: Attackers leveraging weaknesses in network devices, operating systems, or applications to gain unauthorized access or control.

- Data Breaches: Incidents where sensitive information is accessed or disclosed without authorization.

- Ransomware: A type of malware that encrypts a victim's data and demands a ransom payment for its decryption.

- Advanced Persistent Threats (APTs): Sophisticated, long-term attacks often carried out by state-sponsored actors or organized cybercriminal groups.

Recognizing these threats is crucial for understanding the rationale behind network security measures and for using tools like Scapy and

Impacket to simulate and test defenses against them.

The Critical Importance of Network Security in Cybersecurity

Network security is not just a component of cybersecurity; it's a foundational pillar upon which much of the digital world relies. Here's why it's so vital:

- Connectivity is Key: Modern systems and applications are heavily interconnected. A compromise in network security can provide attackers with access to vast amounts of data and critical infrastructure.

- Data in Transit: A significant portion of sensitive data travels across networks. Robust network security measures are essential to protect this data from interception and manipulation.

- Access Point for Attacks: Networks often serve as the primary entry point for cyberattacks. Securing the network perimeter and internal network segments is crucial for preventing breaches.

- Foundation for Other Security Layers: Many other security controls, such as endpoint security and application security, rely on a secure underlying network infrastructure.

- Business Continuity: Network disruptions caused by security incidents can lead to significant financial losses and operational downtime. Strong network security helps ensure business continuity.

- Regulatory Compliance: Many industries and governments have regulations mandating specific network security controls to protect sensitive data.

- Trust and Reputation: Security breaches can erode customer trust and damage an organization's reputation. Strong network security helps maintain trust and protect brand image.

- Enabling Secure Communication: Secure protocols and technologies enable confidential and reliable communication, which is essential for e-commerce, online banking, and many other online activities.

Without robust network security, all other cybersecurity efforts are significantly weakened. It's the frontline defense and the secure highway upon which our digital interactions depend.

Essential Best Practices for Network Security

Implementing effective network security requires a layered approach and adherence to established best practices. Here are some key principles:

- Implement a Strong Firewall: Deploy and properly configure firewalls at the network perimeter and potentially within internal network segments to control traffic flow based on defined rules.

- Deploy Intrusion Detection and Prevention Systems (IDS/IPS): Monitor network traffic for malicious patterns and automatically block or alert on suspicious activity.
- Enforce Strong Authentication and Authorization: Implement robust password policies, multi-factor authentication (MFA) wherever possible, and role-based access control (RBAC) to limit access to resources based on user roles and responsibilities.
- Practice the Principle of Least Privilege: Grant users and systems only the minimum level of access necessary to perform their required tasks.
- Segment Your Network: Divide the network into isolated segments to limit the blast radius of a security incident.
- Secure Wireless Networks: Use strong encryption protocols (WPA3), change default credentials, and consider using MAC

address filtering or captive portals for access control.

- Implement VPNs for Remote Access: Use VPNs to create secure tunnels for remote users accessing the network.

- Keep Systems and Devices Updated: Regularly patch operating systems, network devices, and applications to address known vulnerabilities.

- Implement Network Monitoring and Logging: Continuously monitor network traffic and maintain comprehensive logs for security analysis and incident response.

- Educate Users: Conduct regular security awareness training to educate users about phishing, social engineering, and other common threats.

- Develop and Implement Security Policies and Procedures: Establish clear guidelines and procedures for network security and ensure they are regularly reviewed and updated.

- Conduct Regular Security Audits and Penetration Testing: Periodically assess the effectiveness of network security controls by conducting vulnerability scans and penetration tests (like those you can perform with Scapy and Impacket, with permission!).

- Implement Data Loss Prevention (DLP) Measures: Employ tools and techniques to prevent sensitive data from leaving the network without authorization.

- Establish a Robust Incident Response Plan: Develop a plan to effectively handle security incidents, including detection, containment, eradication, recovery, and lessons learned.

By understanding these fundamental network security concepts, recognizing the threats, and implementing these best practices, you'll be well-equipped to build and maintain more secure network environments. This knowledge provides the essential context for the practical skills you've been developing with Scapy and Impacket, allowing you to apply them effectively in real-world cybersecurity scenarios.

Chapter 10: Penetration Testing with Scapy and Impacket

Welcome to the culmination of our journey! In this chapter, we'll transition from theoretical knowledge and individual tool exploration to real-world application. You'll learn how to combine the power of Scapy and Impacket to conduct effective penetration testing exercises and network security assessments. Get ready to see these tools in action as we simulate attack scenarios and identify potential weaknesses in target environments (remembering to always do so ethically and with explicit permission!).

Hands-on Project: Network Reconnaissance and Vulnerability Scanning

Let's embark on a practical project that integrates both Scapy and Impacket to simulate the initial phases of a penetration test: network reconnaissance and basic vulnerability scanning.

Scenario: You have been authorized to assess the security of a small network segment (e.g., 192.168.1.0/24). Your goal is to identify active hosts, open ports, and potential vulnerabilities using Scapy for network probing and Impacket for interacting with identified services.

Steps:

1. Host Discovery with Scapy (ARP Scan):
    - Use Scapy to send ARP requests to all IP addresses in the target network segment.
    - Analyze the ARP replies to identify active hosts and their MAC addresses.
    - *Python Code Snippet:* (Building upon Chapter 4 example)
    - Python

```python
from scapy.all import Ether, ARP, srp

target_network = "192.168.1.0/24"
arp_request = Ether(dst="ff:ff:ff:ff:ff:ff")/ARP(pdst=target_network)
answered, unanswered = srp(arp_request, timeout=2, verbose=0)

print("Active hosts on the network:")
active_hosts = {}
for sent, received in answered:
    active_hosts[received.psrc] = received.hwsrc
        print(f"IP: {received.psrc} - MAC: {received.hwsrc}")
```

- o
- o

2. Port Scanning with Scapy (TCP SYN Scan):
    o For each identified active host, use Scapy to perform a TCP SYN scan on

a range of common ports (e.g., 21, 22, 23, 80, 135, 139, 443, 445).

- ○ Analyze the SYN-ACK responses to identify open TCP ports.
- ○ *Python Code Snippet (Iterating through active hosts):*
- ○ Python

```python
from scapy.all import IP, TCP, sr1

open_ports = {}
common_ports = [21, 22, 23, 80, 135, 139, 443, 445]

for ip in active_hosts:
    open_ports[ip] = []
    for port in common_ports:
        syn_packet = IP(dst=ip)/TCP(dport=port, flags="S")
```

```python
        response = sr1(syn_packet, timeout=0.5,
verbose=0)
        if response and response.haslayer(TCP) and
response.getlayer(TCP).flags == "SA":
        open_ports[ip].append(port)
    if open_ports[ip]:
        print(f"Open TCP ports on {ip}:
{open_ports[ip]}")
```
    ○

    ○

3. Service Interaction with Impacket (SMB
   Enumeration):
   ○ For hosts with open SMB ports (139
     or 445), use Impacket's
     SMBConnection to attempt to
     connect anonymously (if allowed) or
     with provided credentials (if available
     in a testing scenario).
   ○ List the available shares on the SMB
     service. This can reveal potential
     access points or sensitive data.

- *Python Code Snippet (Iterating through hosts with open SMB ports):*
- Python

```python
from impacket import smb
from socket import gethostbyname

for ip, ports in open_ports.items():
    if 139 in ports or 445 in ports:
        try:
            conn = smb.SMB(ip, '\\\\' + gethostbyname(ip), timeout=1)
            shares = conn.listShares()
            print(f"\nSMB Shares on {ip}:")
            for share in shares:
                print(f" - {share['shi1_netname']}")
            conn.close()
        except Exception as e:
            print(f"Error connecting to SMB on {ip}: {e}")
```

- o
- o

4. Service Interaction with Impacket (Null Session MSRPC Enumeration):

   - o For hosts with open MSRPC port 135, attempt to connect to the samr (Security Account Manager Remote Protocol) service using a null session (no credentials).
   - o Enumerate users or groups if anonymous access is allowed. This can provide valuable information for potential attacks.
   - o *Python Code Snippet (Iterating through active hosts and checking for port 135):*
   - o Python

```
from impacket.dcerpc.v5 import samr
```

```python
from impacket.dcerpc.v5.transport import DCERPCTransportFactory

for ip in active_hosts:
    if 135 in open_ports.get(ip, []):
        stringBinding = r"ncacn_ip_tcp:" + ip + r"[135]"
        try:
            rpctransport = DCERPCTransportFactory(stringBinding)
            dce = rpctransport.get_dce_rpc()
            dce.connect()
            dce.bind(samr.MSRPC_UUID_SAMR)

            resp = samr.SamrEnumerateDomains(dce)
            if resp['Count'] > 0:
                print(f"\nDomains on {ip}:")
                for i in range(resp['Count']):
                    domain_sid = resp['Domains'][i]['Sid']
```

```
                    domain_name =
samr.SamrLookupDomainName(dce,
domain_sid)['Name']
                        print(f"   - SID:
{domain_sid.formatCanonical()},        Name:
{domain_name}")


    dce.disconnect()
  except Exception as e:
        print(f"Error interacting with SAMR on
{ip}: {e}")
        o

        o
```

This project demonstrates how to combine Scapy for low-level network probing and Impacket for higher-level service interaction to gather information about a target network. This information is crucial in the initial stages of a penetration test.

Using Scapy and Impacket for Network Security Testing and Vulnerability Assessment

Beyond basic reconnaissance, Scapy and Impacket can be used for more targeted security testing and vulnerability assessment:

- Firewall Testing (Scapy): Craft packets with specific flags, source/destination ports, and IP addresses to test firewall rules and identify potential bypasses. For example, sending fragmented packets or packets with unusual flag combinations.

- IDS/IPS Evasion (Scapy): Experiment with packet fragmentation, out-of-order delivery, or subtle variations in protocol headers to see if intrusion detection/prevention systems can still identify malicious patterns.

- Authentication Testing (Impacket): Use Impacket's authentication implementations (NTLM, Kerberos) to test the strength and configuration of authentication mechanisms. This includes attempting password spraying, exploiting Kerberos vulnerabilities like AS-REP Roasting, or testing for NTLM relay vulnerabilities.

- Vulnerability Exploitation (Scapy & Impacket): In some cases, you can use Scapy to craft specific exploit packets targeting known network protocol vulnerabilities. Impacket can then be used to interact with the vulnerable service to trigger the exploit. However, exploit development is an advanced topic and requires a deep understanding of the vulnerability.

- Denial-of-Service (DoS) Testing (Scapy): Generate high volumes of specific types of traffic (e.g., SYN floods) using Scapy to test the resilience of target systems to DoS attacks. Use this with extreme caution and only with explicit permission in a controlled environment.

- Application Layer Testing (Scapy & Impacket): Craft and send custom application layer packets (e.g., HTTP requests with malicious payloads using Scapy, or interacting with web services using Impacket's HTTP capabilities) to test for vulnerabilities like command injection or cross-site scripting (XSS).

- Wireless Security Testing (Scapy): Craft and inject wireless frames for tasks like testing WEP/WPA/WPA2 security, performing deauthentication attacks (for testing access point resilience), and analyzing wireless traffic.

Remember that ethical considerations and legal authorization are paramount when conducting any form of penetration testing or vulnerability assessment. Always ensure you have explicit permission before testing any systems that you do not own or have been authorized to assess.

By combining the low-level packet manipulation of Scapy with the high-level protocol interaction of

Impacket, you gain a powerful and flexible toolkit for comprehensively assessing the security of networks and systems. The possibilities are vast, and with continued learning and practice, you can become proficient in using these tools to identify and address security weaknesses.

This chapter serves as a stepping stone towards applying your knowledge in real-world cybersecurity scenarios. Keep exploring, keep learning, and always practice ethical hacking!

Chapter 11: Advanced Penetration Testing Techniques

Welcome to the cutting edge of penetration testing with Scapy and Impacket! In this chapter, we'll explore advanced techniques that go beyond standard scanning and enumeration. You'll learn how to orchestrate more complex attack scenarios, manipulate network protocols in nuanced ways, and even gain insights into how these tools can be used for the intricate work of exploit development and vulnerability research. Prepare to push the boundaries of your cybersecurity skills!

Orchestrating Advanced Penetration Testing Scenarios

Combining Scapy and Impacket allows for the creation of sophisticated attack simulations that mimic real-world threats. Here are some advanced penetration testing techniques you can explore:

- Man-in-the-Middle (MITM) Attacks:
  - ARP Spoofing with Scapy: Use Scapy to craft and send ARP replies that poison the ARP caches of target hosts and the gateway, allowing you to intercept network traffic.
  - Traffic Interception and Manipulation with Scapy: Once in a MITM position, use Scapy to capture network traffic and potentially modify packets on the fly before forwarding them. This can be used for injecting malicious content or eavesdropping on sensitive communications.
  - Leveraging Impacket for Protocol-Specific Attacks over MITM: After establishing a MITM position with Scapy, use Impacket to

perform protocol-specific attacks on intercepted traffic, such as SMB relay or exploiting vulnerabilities in intercepted HTTP requests.

- Advanced Authentication Bypass Techniques:
  - Pass-the-Hash with Impacket: Utilize Impacket's SMB and other protocol implementations to authenticate to systems using NTLM hashes instead of plaintext passwords, demonstrating lateral movement possibilities.
  - Pass-the-Ticket with Impacket: Employ Impacket's Kerberos capabilities to inject stolen Kerberos tickets for authentication, bypassing standard password-based access controls.
  - Kerberoasting and Golden/Silver Ticket Attacks with Impacket: Use Impacket tools to exploit Kerberos

vulnerabilities to obtain service principal names (SPNs) and forge Kerberos tickets, allowing for privileged access within a Windows domain.

- Exploiting Network Protocol Vulnerabilities:
  - Crafting Exploits with Scapy for Low-Level Protocols: For vulnerabilities in lower-level protocols (e.g., specific TCP/IP implementations), Scapy can be used to craft precisely malformed packets to trigger the vulnerability. This often requires deep protocol knowledge and understanding of the target vulnerability.
  - Leveraging Impacket for Higher-Level Protocol Exploits: For vulnerabilities in protocols like SMB, MSRPC, or specific application-layer protocols,

Impacket's protocol implementations can be used to construct exploit payloads and interact with the vulnerable service.

- Advanced Evasion Techniques:
  - Fragmented Attacks with Scapy: Crafting and sending fragmented packets that might bypass or confuse firewalls and intrusion detection systems.
  - Out-of-Order Packet Delivery with Scapy: Sending packets in an unexpected sequence to see if security devices can reassemble and analyze them correctly.
  - Protocol Anomaly Exploitation with Scapy: Deviating from standard protocol behavior in subtle ways to identify weaknesses in how systems handle non-standard traffic.
- Automation of Complex Attack Sequences:

○ Scripting with Python to Coordinate Scapy and Impacket: Write Python scripts that orchestrate a series of actions using both Scapy and Impacket. For example, perform network reconnaissance with Scapy, identify a vulnerable service, and then use Impacket to exploit that service.

Utilizing Scapy and Impacket for Exploit Development and Vulnerability Research

Scapy and Impacket are not just for running existing penetration testing tools; they can also be invaluable assets in the process of discovering new vulnerabilities and developing exploits:

- Fuzzing Network Protocols with Scapy:
  - Generating Malformed Packets: Use Scapy to systematically generate a wide range of malformed or

unexpected packets for various network protocols.

- ○ Monitoring Target Behavior: Send these fuzzed packets to a target system and monitor its behavior (e.g., crashes, unexpected responses) to identify potential vulnerabilities.

- Analyzing Protocol Implementations with Impacket:
  - ○ Dissecting Protocol Structures: Impacket's object-oriented representation of network protocols allows researchers to easily examine the structure and fields of various protocol messages.
  - ○ Identifying Deviations from Standards: By comparing Impacket's implementation with official protocol specifications, researchers can identify potential areas where other

implementations might deviate and introduce vulnerabilities.

- Developing Proof-of-Concept Exploits:
  - Crafting Exploit Payloads with Scapy: For vulnerabilities that can be triggered at the packet level, Scapy can be used to craft the specific sequence of bytes needed to exploit the flaw.
  - Interacting with Vulnerable Services with Impacket: For vulnerabilities in higher-level services, Impacket can be used to establish connections, send malicious requests, and interact with the service in a way that triggers the vulnerability.
- Reverse Engineering Network Protocols:
  - Capturing and Analyzing Traffic with Scapy: Use Scapy to capture network traffic generated by proprietary or less-documented protocols.

- Reconstructing Protocol Structures with Python and Impacket: Analyze the captured traffic and use Python and potentially extend Impacket to understand and interact with these protocols, which can be crucial for identifying security weaknesses.

Important Considerations for Exploit Development and Vulnerability Research:

- Deep Technical Understanding: This area requires a very strong understanding of network protocols, operating systems, and software vulnerabilities.
- Ethical Responsibility: Vulnerability research must be conducted ethically and responsibly. Disclose any discovered vulnerabilities to the vendor in a responsible manner.

- Legal Boundaries: Be aware of and adhere to all applicable laws and regulations regarding vulnerability research and exploitation.
- Controlled Environments: All exploit development and testing should be performed in isolated and controlled lab environments to prevent harm to production systems.

This chapter has provided a glimpse into the advanced capabilities of Scapy and Impacket in the realm of penetration testing and even vulnerability research. Mastering these techniques requires significant dedication and practice, but the ability to orchestrate complex attacks, analyze protocols deeply, and potentially contribute to the discovery of new vulnerabilities is a highly valuable skill in the cybersecurity field. Continue to explore, experiment responsibly, and deepen your understanding of these powerful tools!

Part 5: Advanced Topics and Best Practices

Chapter 12: Advanced Cybersecurity Topics

Welcome to the strategic level of cybersecurity! In this final chapter, we'll explore advanced concepts that are crucial for a holistic security posture. We'll delve into the realms of threat intelligence and incident response, understanding their importance and how your Python, Scapy, and Impacket skills can be leveraged for sophisticated cybersecurity tasks within these domains. Get ready to see the bigger picture and your role within it!

Exploring Advanced Topics in Cybersecurity

Beyond the technical deep dives into network protocols and tools, cybersecurity encompasses broader strategic and operational aspects. Let's explore two key advanced topics:

- Threat Intelligence: This involves the collection, processing, analysis, and dissemination of information about current and potential threats to an organization's security. Effective threat intelligence helps organizations understand the threat landscape, anticipate attacks, and proactively strengthen their defenses. Key aspects of threat intelligence include:
  - Threat Actors: Identifying who is attacking (e.g., nation-state actors, cybercriminal groups, hacktivists), their motivations, capabilities, and common tactics, techniques, and procedures (TTPs).
  - Threat Vectors: Understanding the methods attackers use to gain access (e.g., phishing emails, malware, software vulnerabilities, social engineering).

- Indicators of Compromise (IOCs): Identifying technical artifacts or observables that indicate a system or network has been compromised (e.g., malicious IP addresses, domain names, file hashes, registry keys).
- Vulnerability Intelligence: Staying informed about known vulnerabilities in software and hardware and their potential impact.
- Contextual Analysis: Understanding the relevance and potential impact of threats to the specific organization and its industry.
- Information Sharing: Collaborating with other organizations and security communities to share threat intelligence and improve collective defense.

- Incident Response (IR): This is the organized approach to addressing and managing the aftermath of a security breach or cyberattack. A well-defined incident response plan helps organizations minimize damage, contain the incident, eradicate the threat, and restore normal operations efficiently. The typical phases of incident response include:

- o Preparation: Establishing policies, procedures, and resources for handling incidents. This includes having well-defined roles, communication channels, and necessary tools.

- o Identification: Detecting and verifying that a security incident has occurred. This often involves monitoring logs, analyzing alerts from security systems, and user reports.

- o Containment: Limiting the scope and impact of the incident. This might involve isolating affected systems, segmenting the network, or disabling compromised accounts.

○ Eradication: Removing the threat and any associated components from the affected systems and network. This could involve removing malware, patching vulnerabilities, or rebuilding compromised systems.

○ Recovery: Restoring affected systems and data to normal operation. This might involve restoring from backups or rebuilding services.

○ Lessons Learned: Reviewing the incident to identify what happened, how the response was handled, and what improvements can be made to prevent future incidents.

Understanding these advanced topics provides a broader context for the technical skills you've developed, showing how they fit into the larger cybersecurity ecosystem.

Leveraging Python, Scapy, and Impacket for Advanced Cybersecurity Tasks

The tools and techniques you've learned throughout this guide can be powerful assets in the realms of threat intelligence and incident response:

- Threat Intelligence Applications:
  - Automating IOC Collection and Analysis (Python): Python can be used to automate the collection of IOCs from various threat intelligence feeds (e.g., APIs, open-source intelligence). You can then use Python libraries to parse, analyze, and correlate this data.
  - Network Traffic Analysis for Threat Detection (Scapy): Scapy can be used to analyze network traffic for patterns associated with known threat actors

or malware. You can write scripts to identify specific packet structures, protocols, or communication patterns that match threat intelligence.

- ○ Simulating Threat Actor TTPs for Security Testing (Scapy & Impacket): By understanding the TTPs of specific threat actors, you can use Scapy and Impacket to simulate their attack methods in a controlled environment to test the effectiveness of your defenses. For example, simulating specific types of lateral movement techniques using Impacket or crafting phishing emails with malicious network traffic using Scapy for training exercises.

- ○ Developing Custom Threat Intelligence Tools (Python, Scapy, Impacket): You can build custom tools using these libraries to automate specific threat intelligence tasks tailored to your organization's needs, such as network traffic analysis for specific malware signatures or automated querying of threat intelligence platforms based on network events captured by Scapy.

- Incident Response Applications:
  - Network Forensics and Analysis (Scapy): During incident response, Scapy can be invaluable for analyzing captured network traffic to understand the attacker's actions, identify compromised systems, and trace the flow of malicious activity. You can write scripts to filter and analyze large packet captures for specific patterns or anomalies.
  - Automating Response Actions (Python & Impacket): Python can be used to automate various incident

response tasks. For example, using Impacket to remotely isolate compromised Windows systems by disabling network shares or terminating malicious processes (with appropriate permissions and caution).

- ○ Log Analysis and Correlation (Python): Python has excellent libraries for parsing and analyzing various log formats. You can write scripts to correlate network traffic captured by Scapy with system logs to gain a more complete picture of a security incident.

- ○ Developing Custom Incident Response Tools (Python, Scapy, Impacket): You can build custom tools to aid in specific incident response tasks, such as automatically extracting IOCs from network traffic captures using Scapy or interacting with compromised systems using Impacket for remediation (again, with extreme caution and proper authorization).

○ Malware Analysis Support (Python & Scapy): While not direct malware analysis tools, Python and Scapy can assist in dynamic malware analysis by capturing and analyzing the network traffic generated by malware in a sandbox environment.

Key Considerations for Advanced Tasks:

- Deep Understanding of Security Principles: Effectively applying these tools in advanced scenarios requires a strong understanding of underlying security principles and attack methodologies.
- Careful Planning and Execution: Advanced tasks, especially in incident response, require

meticulous planning and careful execution to avoid causing further damage or disrupting legitimate operations.

- Ethical Considerations and Legal Compliance: Always ensure that your actions are ethical and comply with all relevant laws and regulations, especially when dealing with live systems or sensitive data.

- Continuous Learning: The cybersecurity landscape is constantly evolving. Staying up-to-date with the latest threats, techniques, and tools is crucial for success in these advanced domains.

This chapter concludes our journey through Python for cybersecurity with Scapy and Impacket. You've gained a solid foundation in network security principles and the practical skills to leverage these powerful tools for a wide range of tasks, from basic network exploration to advanced penetration testing and even contributing to threat intelligence and incident response efforts. The path of a cybersecurity professional is one of continuous learning and adaptation. Keep practicing, keep exploring, and always strive to use your knowledge to make the digital world a safer place. Good luck on your cybersecurity endeavors!

Chapter 13: Best Practices for Cybersecurity Professionals

Welcome to the guiding principles of our profession! In this concluding chapter, we'll step back from the specific tools and techniques and focus on the broader best practices that should underpin your journey as a cybersecurity professional. We'll explore the ethical considerations, continuous learning imperatives, and collaborative spirit that are essential for navigating the complex and dynamic landscape of cybersecurity. This chapter is about cultivating not just technical skills, but also the mindset of an effective and responsible security practitioner.

Essential Best Practices for Cybersecurity Professionals

Being a successful cybersecurity professional involves more than just technical prowess. It requires a strong ethical compass, a commitment to continuous learning, and the ability to collaborate effectively. Here are some essential best practices to guide your career:

- Uphold Ethical Standards: Integrity and ethical behavior are paramount in cybersecurity. Always operate within legal and ethical boundaries, respect privacy, and obtain proper authorization before conducting any security assessments or testing. Transparency and honesty in your work are crucial for building trust.
- Practice Responsible Disclosure: If you discover vulnerabilities, follow responsible disclosure practices. This typically involves reporting the vulnerability to the affected vendor in a private and timely manner, allowing them a reasonable timeframe to address the issue before public disclosure.

- Prioritize Continuous Learning: The cybersecurity landscape is constantly changing, with new threats, vulnerabilities, and technologies emerging regularly. Commit to lifelong learning through continuous education, certifications, attending conferences, reading industry publications, and participating in online communities.
- Stay Updated on Threats and Trends: Actively monitor current cybersecurity trends, emerging threats, and the latest attack techniques. Understanding the evolving threat landscape is crucial for proactive defense and effective security assessments.
- Develop Strong Communication Skills: Cybersecurity professionals need to communicate effectively with technical and non-technical audiences. Clearly explain complex security concepts, risks, and

recommendations in a way that is understandable to stakeholders.

- Document Your Work Thoroughly: Maintain detailed and accurate documentation of your methodologies, findings, and recommendations. This is essential for reproducibility, collaboration, and providing clear reports.

- Collaborate and Share Knowledge: Cybersecurity is a team sport. Collaborate with colleagues, share knowledge, and contribute to the broader security community. Participate in forums, share insights, and learn from others' experiences.

- Understand Business Context: Security decisions should align with business goals and risk tolerance. Understand the organization's objectives and tailor your security recommendations accordingly.

- Focus on Risk Management: Cybersecurity is ultimately about managing risk. Learn to identify, assess, and prioritize security risks and recommend appropriate mitigation strategies.

- Embrace Automation: Leverage scripting and automation (using Python, for example) to streamline repetitive tasks, improve efficiency, and enhance the scalability of your security efforts.

- Think Like an Attacker (Ethically): To effectively defend systems, you need to understand how attackers think and operate. Emulate attack scenarios (with permission!) to identify potential weaknesses.

- Practice Defense in Depth: Implement a layered security approach, where multiple security controls are in place. If one layer fails, others can still provide protection.

- Respect Privacy and Data Protection: Handle sensitive data with the utmost care and adhere to relevant privacy regulations and best practices for data protection.

- Be Proactive, Not Just Reactive: Aim to anticipate potential threats and implement preventative measures rather than solely responding to incidents.
- Develop Problem-Solving Skills: Cybersecurity professionals are constantly faced with complex challenges. Cultivate strong analytical and problem-solving skills to effectively diagnose and resolve security issues.

The Paramount Importance of Staying Up-to-Date with Cybersecurity Trends and Threats

In the dynamic world of cybersecurity, stagnation is akin to falling behind. The threat landscape evolves rapidly, with attackers constantly developing new techniques and exploiting emerging vulnerabilities. Here's why staying current is absolutely critical:

- Emerging Threats: New types of malware, attack vectors, and social engineering tactics are constantly being developed. Staying informed allows you to recognize and defend against these novel threats.

- Evolving Attack Techniques: Attackers continuously refine their methods to bypass existing security controls. Understanding these evolving techniques is crucial for adapting your defenses and testing methodologies.

- New Vulnerabilities: Software and hardware vulnerabilities are discovered regularly. Staying updated on these vulnerabilities and their potential impact is essential for timely patching and mitigation.

- Changes in Technology: The introduction of new technologies (e.g., cloud computing, IoT, AI) brings new security challenges and requires new skills and knowledge.

- Shifting Regulatory Landscape: Data privacy laws and security regulations are constantly evolving. Staying informed ensures compliance and helps avoid legal repercussions.

- Improved Tools and Techniques: New security tools and techniques are developed to counter emerging threats. Continuous learning allows you to leverage these advancements to improve your effectiveness.
- Understanding the Adversary: Threat intelligence provides insights into the motivations, capabilities, and TTPs of different threat actors. Staying updated on this intelligence helps you anticipate and attribute attacks.
- Maintaining Relevance and Value: In a rapidly changing field, continuous learning ensures that your skills and knowledge remain relevant and valuable to your organization and the broader cybersecurity community.

How to Stay Up-to-Date:

- Follow Reputable Security News Sources: Subscribe to blogs, news websites, and social media accounts of trusted cybersecurity organizations and professionals.
- Read Industry Publications and Research Papers: Stay informed about in-depth research and analysis of emerging threats and trends.
- Attend Conferences and Webinars: Participate in industry events to learn from experts, network with peers, and stay abreast of the latest developments.
- Engage in Online Communities: Participate in forums, mailing lists, and social media groups focused on cybersecurity to exchange knowledge and learn from others.
- Pursue Continuous Education and Certifications: Obtain relevant certifications and take courses to deepen your knowledge in specific areas of cybersecurity.

- Experiment in Lab Environments: Continuously practice and experiment with new tools and techniques in a safe and controlled lab environment.
- Contribute to Open Source Projects: Engaging with open-source security projects can provide hands-on experience with cutting-edge technologies and foster collaboration.

The journey of a cybersecurity professional is a marathon, not a sprint. By embracing these best practices and committing to continuous learning, you will not only become a more effective practitioner but also contribute to a more secure digital world.

The skills you've gained with Python, Scapy, and Impacket are powerful tools in your arsenal, and by combining them with a strong ethical foundation and a thirst for knowledge, you are well-equipped to make a significant impact in the field of cybersecurity. Keep learning, stay curious, and be a force for good in the digital realm!

Chapter 14: Troubleshooting and Debugging

Welcome to the problem-solving toolkit! In this chapter, we'll focus on the practical art of troubleshooting and debugging when working with Scapy and Impacket. No matter how well you understand these tools, you'll inevitably encounter situations where things don't go as planned. We'll explore systematic approaches and common pitfalls, providing you with the strategies and techniques to diagnose and resolve issues efficiently. This chapter is about empowering you to become a resourceful and independent problem-solver in your cybersecurity endeavors.

Systematic Troubleshooting and Debugging Techniques

When faced with an issue in your Scapy or Impacket scripts, a structured approach can save you significant time and frustration. Here's a general methodology to follow:

1. Understand the Error: Carefully read any error messages or exceptions you encounter. Pay attention to the traceback in Python, as it often pinpoints the exact line of code where the problem occurred and provides clues about the nature of the error.

2. Isolate the Problem: Try to narrow down the source of the issue. If you have a complex script, comment out sections of code to identify the specific part that's causing the problem. Simplify your script to the bare minimum required to reproduce the error.

3. Reproduce the Error Consistently: Ensure that you can consistently reproduce the error. This will help you verify if your fixes are actually working.

4. Gather Information: Collect as much information as possible about the context in which the error occurs. This might include:

   o Your operating system and Python version.

   o The versions of Scapy and Impacket you are using.

   o The network environment you are working in.

   o The specific commands or functions you are using.

   o The target system you are interacting with (if applicable).

5. Consult Documentation and Resources: Refer to the official documentation for Scapy and Impacket. Look for examples, tutorials, and troubleshooting guides. Online forums, Stack Overflow, and the libraries' GitHub issue trackers can also be valuable resources for finding solutions to common problems.

6. Use Print Statements Strategically: Insert print() statements at various points in your code to inspect the values of variables, the flow of execution, and the content of packets or protocol objects. This can help you understand what's happening at each step.

7. Leverage Debugging Tools: Python's built-in debugger (pdb) can be incredibly useful for stepping through your code line by line, inspecting variables, and understanding the program's state at any given point. Consider using IDEs with integrated debugging features.

8. Test Incrementally: When making changes to your code to fix an issue, test frequently and in small increments. This makes it easier to identify which change resolved the problem (or introduced a new one).

9. Seek Help When Needed: If you've exhausted your troubleshooting efforts, don't hesitate to ask for help from online

communities or colleagues. When asking for help, provide as much detail as possible about the problem, the steps you've taken, and any error messages you've encountered.

Common Issues and Best Practices for Resolution (Scapy)

Here are some common issues you might encounter when using Scapy and best practices for resolving them:

- Permission Errors (Sending/Sniffing):
  - Issue: socket.error: [Errno 1] Operation not permitted or similar errors when trying to send or sniff packets.
  - Resolution: Sending and sniffing raw packets often requires root or administrator privileges. Ensure you are running your Python script or the Scapy interactive shell with the

necessary elevated permissions (e.g., using sudo on Linux, running as Administrator on Windows).

- Interface Not Found:
  - Issue: Errors indicating that the specified network interface does not exist.
  - Resolution: Use scapy.all.get_if_list() to list available network interfaces on your system and ensure you are using the correct interface name in your send(), sendp(), or sniff() calls (e.g., iface="eth0" on Linux, iface="Ethernet0" on Windows).
- Packets Not Sent or Received:
  - Issue: Your crafted packets are not reaching the destination, or you are not receiving expected responses.
  - Resolution:
    - Firewall Interference: Local firewalls on your system or the

target system might be blocking the packets. Temporarily disable firewalls for testing (with caution and in authorized environments).

- Incorrect Layering or Fields: Double-check the layers you've added to your packets and the values of the fields you've set using packet.show(). Ensure they conform to the protocol specifications.

- Routing Issues: Verify that your system has a route to the target network using route -n (Linux) or route print (Windows).

- Incorrect Destination Address: Ensure the destination IP and MAC addresses are correct. For ARP requests, the target IP (pdst) should be in the same local network segment.

- Layer 2 vs. Layer 3 Sending: Use send() for layer 3 (IP and above) and sendp() for layer 2 (Ethernet). Ensure you are using the appropriate function for the layers you've constructed.

- Unexpected Sniffing Results:
  - Issue: You are capturing too many packets or not the specific traffic you are interested in.
  - Resolution: Use the filter parameter in the sniff() function to specify Berkeley Packet Filter (BPF) syntax to narrow down the captured traffic (e.g., filter="tcp port 80" to capture only HTTP traffic).
- Scapy Not Installed or Import Errors:

- Issue: ImportError: No module named 'scapy' or similar errors.
- Resolution: Ensure Scapy is correctly installed in your Python environment. Try reinstalling it using pip install scapy or pip3 install scapy.

Common Issues and Best Practices for Resolution (Impacket)

Here are some common issues you might encounter when using Impacket and best practices for resolving them:

- Connection Errors:
  - Issue: Unable to establish a connection to the target service (e.g., SMB, MSRPC, LDAP).
  - Resolution:
    - Incorrect Hostname or IP Address: Double-check the target hostname or IP address.

- Firewall Blocking: Firewalls on your system or the target system might be blocking the connection on the required port (e.g., 445 for SMB, 135 for MSRPC, 389 for LDAP).
- Service Not Running: Ensure the target service is running on the remote host.
- Incorrect Protocol or Port: Verify that you are using the correct protocol and port for the service you are trying to connect to.

- Authentication Errors:
  - Issue: Unable to authenticate to the target service.
  - Resolution:
    - Incorrect Credentials: Double-check the username and password you are using.

- Domain Issues: For domain-joined systems, ensure you are providing the correct domain information.
- Authentication Protocol Mismatch: Some services might require specific authentication protocols (e.g., NTLMv1 vs. NTLMv2, Kerberos). Ensure your Impacket code is using a compatible protocol.
- Account Lockout: Repeated failed login attempts might lead to account lockout.
- Protocol-Specific Errors:
  - Issue: Errors related to specific protocols (e.g., SMB, MSRPC, LDAP).
  - Resolution:

- Consult Protocol Documentation: Refer to the documentation for the specific protocol you are working with to understand the expected message formats and error codes.

- Examine Impacket Source Code: Sometimes, looking at the Impacket source code for the specific protocol implementation can provide insights into expected behavior and potential issues.

- Use Network Analysis Tools: Use Wireshark to capture and analyze the network traffic exchanged during the Impacket interaction. This can help you see the raw protocol messages and identify discrepancies.

- Impacket Not Installed or Import Errors:
  - Issue: ImportError: No module named 'impacket' or similar errors.
  - Resolution: Ensure Impacket is correctly installed in your Python environment. Try reinstalling it using pip install impacket or by following the installation instructions in the Impacket documentation (which might involve cloning the repository and installing dependencies).

By adopting a systematic approach to troubleshooting and familiarizing yourself with these common issues and their resolutions, you'll become more adept at overcoming challenges and effectively utilizing Scapy and Impacket in your cybersecurity endeavors.

Remember that persistence and a methodical mindset are key to successful debugging.

Part 6: Conclusion and Next Steps

Chapter 15: Case Studies in Cybersecurity

Welcome to the world of practical application! In this chapter, we'll move beyond theoretical examples and explore real-world scenarios where Python, Scapy, and Impacket have been instrumental in tackling significant cybersecurity challenges. By examining these case studies and the insights shared by industry experts, you'll gain a deeper appreciation for the power and versatility of these tools in addressing complex security issues and learn valuable lessons for your own cybersecurity journey.

Real-World Case Studies: Python, Scapy, and Impacket in Action

These case studies illustrate how the tools you've learned about are applied in various cybersecurity domains:

- Case Study 1: Network Intrusion Detection System (NIDS) Development with Scapy:
    - Scenario: A security team needed to develop a custom NIDS to detect specific types of network attacks that off-the-shelf solutions were not effectively identifying.
    - Implementation: They used Scapy to sniff network traffic in real-time and implemented custom packet analysis rules in Python. Scapy's ability to dissect packets at various layers allowed them to identify specific patterns indicative of malicious activity, such as unusual flag combinations in TCP packets, malformed headers, or specific payload content. Python's scripting

capabilities enabled them to automate the analysis and alerting process.

- Lessons Learned: The flexibility of Scapy allowed for the detection of sophisticated, custom attacks. The importance of deep protocol understanding for crafting effective detection rules was highlighted. Real-time processing of network traffic required careful optimization of Python code for performance.[1]

- Case Study 2: Automated Vulnerability Assessment of Windows Environments with Impacket:
  - Scenario: A penetration testing team needed to efficiently assess the security posture of a large Windows-based network.
  - Implementation: They leveraged Impacket's extensive support for Windows protocols like SMB and

MSRPC to automate various vulnerability checks.[2] This included testing for weak SMB configurations, attempting null session connections to enumerate users and shares, and identifying vulnerable MSRPC services. Python scripting was used to orchestrate these checks across multiple target systems and generate comprehensive reports.

- ○ Lessons Learned: Impacket significantly streamlined the process of auditing Windows environments. The ability to programmatically interact with Windows services allowed for more thorough and efficient testing compared to manual methods. Proper credential management and ethical considerations were paramount when automating these assessments.

- Case Study 3: Development of a Custom Network Fuzzer with Scapy for Protocol Testing:
  - Scenario: A security research team wanted to test the robustness of a proprietary network protocol implementation against malformed inputs.
  - Implementation: They used Scapy to craft a wide range of valid and invalid packets for the target protocol, systematically varying header fields and payload content. Python was used to automate the packet generation and transmission process. The team monitored the target system for crashes or unexpected behavior to identify potential vulnerabilities.
  - Lessons Learned: Scapy's flexibility in crafting arbitrary packets made it ideal for protocol fuzzing.[3] Understanding

the target protocol's specifications was crucial for designing effective fuzzing strategies. Careful monitoring and analysis of the target system's response were essential for identifying vulnerabilities.

- Case Study 4: Incident Response and Network Forensics with Scapy:
    - Scenario: A security incident involving suspicious network traffic was detected. The incident response team needed to analyze captured network data to understand the attacker's actions.
    - Implementation: They used Scapy to parse and analyze the captured PCAP files. Python scripting allowed them to filter and correlate network traffic based on various criteria (e.g., IP addresses, ports, protocols, specific payloads).[4] This helped them

reconstruct the attacker's communication patterns, identify compromised hosts, and extract indicators of compromise.

- Lessons Learned: Scapy's ability to dissect and analyze network traffic at a granular level was invaluable for incident response and forensics.[5] Python's scripting capabilities enabled efficient processing of large datasets.[6] A deep understanding of network protocols was essential for interpreting the captured traffic effectively.

- Case Study 5: Building a Threat Intelligence Aggregation Tool with Python:
  - Scenario: A security operations center (SOC) needed to aggregate and analyze threat intelligence data from multiple sources.

- Implementation: They used Python to build a tool that could fetch data from various threat intelligence feeds (APIs, flat files, etc.), parse the information, and store it in a centralized database. Python's libraries for web requests, data parsing (e.g., JSON, XML), and database interaction were crucial for this project.
- Lessons Learned: Python's versatility and extensive libraries made it well-suited for building custom threat intelligence tools.[7] Automation of data collection and analysis significantly improved the efficiency of the SOC. The ability to integrate data from diverse sources provided a more comprehensive view of the threat landscape.

Lessons Learned and Best Practices from Industry Experts

Based on real-world experiences, here are some key lessons learned and best practices when using Python, Scapy, and Impacket in cybersecurity projects:

- Master the Fundamentals: A strong foundation in Python and network protocols is essential for effectively using Scapy and Impacket. Don't skip the basics.
- Understand the Tools Deeply: Take the time to truly understand the capabilities and limitations of Scapy and Impacket. Experiment and explore their features beyond basic examples.
- Focus on Specific Problems: Don't try to solve everything at once. Break down complex cybersecurity challenges into smaller, manageable tasks that can be addressed with targeted scripts using these tools.

- Automate Repetitive Tasks: Leverage Python's scripting capabilities to automate routine tasks like network scanning, data collection, and report generation.[8] This saves time and improves efficiency.

- Prioritize Clarity and Readability: Write clean, well-documented Python code. This makes it easier to maintain, collaborate on, and troubleshoot your scripts.

- Handle Errors Gracefully: Implement robust error handling in your scripts to prevent unexpected crashes and provide informative feedback.

- Test Thoroughly in Controlled Environments: Always test your scripts and tools in isolated lab environments before using them on live networks. This helps prevent unintended consequences.

- Be Ethical and Legal: Always operate within ethical and legal boundaries. Obtain proper authorization before conducting any security assessments or testing.

- Combine Tools Strategically: Understand when to use Scapy for low-level packet manipulation and Impacket for higher-level protocol interaction. Combining their strengths can lead to more effective solutions.
- Stay Updated: The cybersecurity landscape and these tools themselves are constantly evolving. Stay current with the latest updates, best practices, and emerging threats.
- Share and Collaborate: Engage with the cybersecurity community, share your knowledge, and learn from the experiences of others. Collaboration can lead to more innovative and effective solutions.
- Think Like an Analyst: When using these tools for analysis (e.g., network forensics, threat intelligence), focus on asking the right

questions and interpreting the data in a meaningful context.

These case studies and expert insights underscore the practical value and versatility of Python, Scapy, and Impacket in addressing a wide range of cybersecurity challenges. By learning from these real-world applications and adhering to best practices, you can effectively leverage these powerful tools in your own cybersecurity journey. Remember that continuous learning and ethical conduct are paramount as you apply these skills in the field.

Chapter 16: Future of Cybersecurity

Welcome to the horizon of cybersecurity! In this concluding chapter, we'll shift our focus from current tools and techniques to the evolving landscape of cyber threats and defenses. We'll explore the key trends shaping the future of cybersecurity and delve into the emerging technologies and innovations that will define how we protect our digital world in the years to come. Understanding these future directions is essential for long-term career growth and strategic planning in this ever-evolving domain.

Future Trends and Directions in Cybersecurity

The cybersecurity landscape is in constant flux, driven by technological advancements and the ever-evolving tactics of cyber adversaries. Here are some key trends and directions to watch:

- Increased Sophistication of Attacks: We will likely see even more sophisticated and targeted attacks leveraging advanced techniques like artificial intelligence (AI), machine learning (ML), and complex social engineering. Attacks will become more personalized and harder to detect.

- Expansion of the Attack Surface: The proliferation of connected devices (IoT), cloud computing, and edge computing will dramatically expand the attack surface, creating more potential entry points for malicious actors. Securing this increasingly complex and distributed environment will be a major challenge.

- Rise of Nation-State and Organized Cybercrime: Nation-state actors and organized cybercriminal groups will continue to pose significant threats, engaging in espionage, sabotage, and ransomware attacks with increasing sophistication and resources.

- Focus on Supply Chain Security: Attacks targeting the software supply chain and third-party vendors will become more prevalent as attackers seek to compromise multiple organizations through a single point of entry.

- Growing Importance of Data Privacy and Compliance: Regulations like GDPR and CCPA will continue to shape how organizations handle and protect personal data, making data privacy and compliance a central focus of cybersecurity efforts.

- Integration of Physical and Cyber Security: The convergence of physical and cyber systems (e.g., in industrial control systems and smart cities) will create new and potentially high-impact security risks.

- Increased Automation in Attacks and Defense: Attackers will increasingly leverage automation for reconnaissance, exploitation, and lateral movement. Simultaneously, AI and ML will play a growing role in automated threat detection, analysis, and response.

- Emphasis on Resilience and Recovery: Recognizing that breaches are inevitable, organizations will place a greater emphasis on building resilient systems and having robust incident response and recovery plans to minimize the impact of successful attacks.

- Talent Shortage and the Need for Skilled Professionals: The cybersecurity skills gap will likely persist, driving demand for qualified professionals with expertise in areas like cloud security, threat intelligence, and incident response.

- Cybersecurity Mesh Architecture: This distributed architectural approach aims to provide scalable and flexible security controls across the expanding digital landscape, focusing on identity-centric security and policy enforcement.

- Zero Trust Security Models: The traditional perimeter-based security model is becoming less effective. The future will see a greater adoption of Zero Trust principles, assuming no user or device is inherently trustworthy and requiring strict verification for every access request.

Emerging Technologies and Innovations in Cybersecurity

To address these evolving threats and challenges, several emerging technologies and innovations are poised to reshape the future of cybersecurity:

- Artificial Intelligence (AI) and Machine Learning (ML):
    - Threat Detection and Analysis: AI/ML algorithms can analyze vast

amounts of security data to identify anomalies, detect sophisticated attacks, and predict future threats with greater accuracy and speed than traditional methods.

- Automated Response: AI-powered systems can automate certain incident response actions, such as isolating infected systems or blocking malicious traffic, allowing for faster and more efficient containment.

- Behavioral Biometrics: AI can analyze user behavior patterns (e.g., typing speed, mouse movements) to detect compromised accounts or insider threats.

- Adversarial AI: Conversely, AI can also be used by attackers to create more sophisticated and evasive attacks, requiring defenders to develop countermeasures.

- Blockchain Technology:
  - Secure Identity Management: Blockchain can provide a decentralized and tamper-proof way to manage digital identities, potentially reducing the risk of identity theft and fraud.
  - Secure Data Sharing: Blockchain can enable secure and auditable data sharing between trusted parties.
  - Supply Chain Security: Blockchain can enhance the transparency and security of supply chains, making it harder for malicious actors to introduce compromised components.
- Quantum Computing:
  - Cryptographic Challenges: While still in its early stages, quantum computing has the potential to break many current encryption algorithms. This necessitates the development and

adoption of post-quantum cryptography.

  ○ Enhanced Threat Analysis: Conversely, quantum computing could potentially be used to accelerate the analysis of complex security data and the development of new defense mechanisms.

- Homomorphic Encryption: This advanced encryption technique allows computations to be performed on encrypted data without decrypting it first, preserving privacy and security in data processing and analysis.
- Confidential Computing: Technologies like Trusted Execution Environments (TEEs) aim to protect sensitive data in use, even if the underlying system is compromised, by creating isolated and secure enclaves for computation.
- Biometric Authentication: Advanced biometric methods (e.g., facial recognition,

fingerprint scanning, iris scanning) offer more secure and user-friendly alternatives to traditional passwords.

- Extended Detection and Response (XDR): XDR solutions integrate security data from endpoints, networks, cloud environments, and email to provide a more holistic and coordinated approach to threat detection and response.

- Security Orchestration, Automation, and Response (SOAR): SOAR platforms automate repetitive security tasks, streamline incident response workflows, and improve the efficiency of security operations teams.

- DevSecOps: Integrating security practices into the software development lifecycle from the beginning ("shifting left") to build more secure applications and infrastructure.

Understanding these future trends and emerging technologies is crucial for cybersecurity professionals to adapt their skills, anticipate future challenges, and contribute to the development and deployment of innovative security solutions. The future of cybersecurity will be shaped by a constant race between evolving threats and cutting-edge defenses, making it a dynamic and intellectually stimulating field to be a part of. As you embark on your cybersecurity journey, remember that continuous learning and an open mind to new possibilities will be your greatest assets in navigating this exciting future.

Chapter 17: Conclusion and Next Steps

Congratulations on reaching the final chapter! This journey has equipped you with a powerful skillset at the intersection of Python programming and cybersecurity, focusing on the potent capabilities of Scapy and Impacket. In this concluding section, we'll recap the essential takeaways from our exploration and chart a course for your continued growth and engagement within the ever-evolving landscape of cybersecurity.

Summary of Key Takeaways from the Book

Throughout this guide, we've covered a significant amount of ground, building your knowledge from foundational cybersecurity concepts to advanced techniques using specialized Python libraries. Here's a summary of the key areas we've explored:

- Cybersecurity Fundamentals: We established a strong understanding of core cybersecurity concepts, the importance of network security, and the historical evolution of cyber threats and defenses.
- Python Essentials for Cybersecurity: We reviewed fundamental Python concepts relevant to our domain, emphasizing best practices for writing secure and efficient security scripts.
- Introduction to Scapy: You were introduced to Scapy's power as an interactive packet manipulation tool, capable of crafting, sending, sniffing, and dissecting network packets across various protocols.
- Scapy Basics and Advanced Topics: You learned to use Scapy for fundamental tasks like crafting and sending packets, network exploration, and advanced techniques such

as custom packet injection and fragmentation.

- Introduction to Impacket: You discovered Impacket, a Python library specializing in higher-level network protocols, particularly those prevalent in Windows environments like SMB and MSRPC.

- Impacket Basics and Advanced Topics: You gained practical skills in using Impacket for network protocol analysis, interacting with services like SMB and MSRPC, and exploring advanced techniques for authentication attacks and remote code execution.

- Network Security Fundamentals: We revisited core network security principles, common threats, and essential best practices for building and maintaining secure network infrastructures.

- Penetration Testing with Scapy and Impacket: You learned how to combine

Scapy and Impacket for practical penetration testing scenarios, including network reconnaissance, vulnerability scanning, and simulating various attack vectors.

- Advanced Penetration Testing Techniques: We explored more sophisticated attack methodologies leveraging the advanced features of both Scapy and Impacket, including MITM attacks and authentication bypass techniques.

- Advanced Cybersecurity Topics: We broadened our scope to include strategic areas like threat intelligence and incident response, discussing how Python, Scapy, and Impacket can be applied in these advanced tasks.

- Best Practices for Cybersecurity Professionals: We emphasized the importance of ethical conduct, continuous learning, strong communication, and collaboration in the cybersecurity field.

- Troubleshooting and Debugging: You gained valuable techniques for identifying and resolving common issues encountered when working with Scapy and Impacket.
- Real-World Case Studies: We examined practical examples of how these tools are used in the industry to solve real cybersecurity challenges.
- Future of Cybersecurity: We explored emerging trends and technologies that will shape the future of the field, highlighting the ongoing need for skilled professionals.

Future Directions and Opportunities in Cybersecurity with Python, Scapy, and Impacket

The skills you've developed throughout this book provide a strong foundation for a wide range of exciting future directions and opportunities within cybersecurity. Here are some potential paths you can explore:

- Advanced Penetration Testing and Red Teaming: Continue to hone your skills in using Scapy and Impacket for more complex penetration testing engagements, including simulating advanced persistent threats (APTs) and developing custom attack tools.
- Network Security Engineering: Apply your knowledge of network protocols and packet analysis to design, implement, and maintain secure network architectures.
- Threat Intelligence Analysis: Leverage Python scripting and your understanding of network traffic to analyze threat data, identify attack patterns, and contribute to proactive defense strategies.
- Incident Response and Forensics: Utilize Scapy for network forensics, analyzing captured traffic to understand security incidents, and use Python and Impacket for automating response actions.

- Security Tool Development: Contribute to or develop your own custom security tools and scripts using Python, Scapy, and Impacket to address specific security needs.
- Vulnerability Research and Exploit Development: With a deep understanding of network protocols and these tools, you can delve into vulnerability research and potentially contribute to the development of exploits (always ethically and responsibly).
- Cloud Security: Apply your networking and security skills to the unique challenges of securing cloud environments, potentially using Python to interact with cloud APIs and analyze network traffic within the cloud.
- IoT Security: As the Internet of Things expands, your ability to analyze network protocols and craft custom packets with Scapy can be invaluable in assessing the security of connected devices.

- Security Automation and Orchestration: Use Python to automate security tasks and orchestrate responses across different security tools and platforms.

Next Steps for Your Journey:

- Continuous Practice: The key to mastery is consistent practice. Continue to experiment with Scapy and Impacket in safe and controlled environments.
- Explore Further Documentation: Dive deeper into the official documentation for Scapy and Impacket to uncover more advanced features and functionalities.
- Contribute to Open Source Projects: Consider contributing to the Scapy or Impacket projects or other open-source security tools. This is a great way to learn from experienced developers and give back to the community.

- Engage with the Cybersecurity Community: Participate in online forums, attend conferences, and network with other cybersecurity professionals.
- Pursue Relevant Certifications: Consider pursuing industry-recognized cybersecurity certifications to validate your skills and enhance your career prospects.
- Build a Portfolio: Showcase your skills by working on personal projects, contributing to open source, or participating in capture-the-flag (CTF) competitions.
- Stay Curious and Keep Learning: The field of cybersecurity is constantly evolving. Maintain a curious mindset and commit to lifelong learning to stay ahead of the curve.

The knowledge and skills you've gained through this book provide a powerful springboard for a successful and impactful career in cybersecurity. Embrace the challenges, continue to learn and grow, and always strive to use your abilities to protect and defend the digital world. The journey is just beginning, and the opportunities are vast. Go forth and make a difference!

Appendices

This section provides supplementary materials and resources to enhance your understanding and practical application of the concepts and tools discussed throughout this book. It includes installation guides, common commands, further reading suggestions, and other helpful references.

Appendix A: Installation Guide for Python, Scapy, and Impacket

- A.1 Installing Python:
  - Step-by-step instructions for installing Python on Windows, macOS, and Linux operating systems.
  - Guidance on setting up virtual environments using venv or conda to manage dependencies effectively.
  - Verification steps to ensure Python is installed correctly.

- A.2 Installing Scapy:
  - Detailed instructions for installing Scapy using pip.
  - Addressing potential dependencies and installation issues on different platforms (e.g., libpcap-dev on Linux).
  - Verification steps to confirm Scapy is installed and functioning correctly, including importing it in the Python interpreter.
- A.3 Installing Impacket:
  - Step-by-step instructions for installing Impacket from PyPI using pip.
  - Alternative installation methods, such as cloning the GitHub repository for development or specific version access.
  - Addressing potential dependencies and installation issues.

○ Verification steps to ensure Impacket is installed and importable in Python.

Appendix B: Common Scapy Commands and Examples

- B.1 Basic Packet Crafting:
    - ○ Examples of crafting common packet types (Ethernet, IP, TCP, UDP, ICMP, ARP).
    - ○ Demonstrating how to set and modify different layer fields.
    - ○ Illustrative code snippets for building custom packets.
- B.2 Sending and Receiving Packets:
    - ○ Examples of using send(), sendp(), sr(), and srp() functions.
    - ○ Demonstrating the use of the iface and timeout parameters.
    - ○ Examples of capturing responses and analyzing the results.

- B.3 Packet Sniffing:
  - Examples of using the sniff() function with various parameters (e.g., count, filter, prn).
  - Illustrating the use of Berkeley Packet Filter (BPF) syntax for targeted traffic capture.
  - Examples of writing callback functions (prn) to process captured packets.
- B.4 Packet Dissection and Analysis:
  - Demonstrating how to access and interpret different layers and fields of captured or crafted packets.
  - Examples of using packet.show() and accessing specific layer attributes.

Appendix C: Common Impacket Usage and Examples

- C.1 SMB Interaction:

- Examples of using SMBConnection to list shares, connect to named pipes, and perform basic file operations.
- Illustrative code snippets for authenticating to SMB services.

- **C.2 MSRPC Interaction:**
  - Examples of using DCERPCTransportFactory to connect to various MSRPC services.
  - Demonstrating how to bind to specific interfaces and call RPC functions (e.g., wkssvc, samr).
  - Illustrative code snippets for retrieving system information or enumerating users (where applicable and authorized).

- **C.3 LDAP Interaction:**
  - Examples of using the ldap module to connect to LDAP servers, authenticate, and perform basic queries.

- Illustrative code snippets for searching for specific objects and retrieving attributes.
- C.4 Authentication Examples:
  - Illustrative code snippets demonstrating the use of NTLM hashes and Kerberos tickets with Impacket.

Appendix D: Further Reading and Resources

- D.1 Books:
  - Recommended books on Python programming for security.
  - Recommended books on network security, penetration testing, and ethical hacking.
  - Recommended books on specific protocols (TCP/IP, SMB, Kerberos, etc.).
- D.2 Online Resources:

- o Links to official documentation for Python, Scapy, and Impacket.
- o Links to relevant online communities, forums, and mailing lists.
- o Links to reputable cybersecurity blogs and news websites.
- o Links to capture-the-flag (CTF) platforms for practical skill development.
- D.3 Tools and Frameworks:
  - o Brief overview of other relevant cybersecurity tools and frameworks that complement Scapy and Impacket.

Appendix E: Glossary of Terms

- A comprehensive glossary of key cybersecurity terms, acronyms, and concepts used throughout the book. This will serve as a quick reference for understanding technical jargon.

This comprehensive appendices section will provide you with the practical guidance and resources you need to continue your learning and effectively apply Python, Scapy, and Impacket in your cybersecurity endeavors. It's designed to be a valuable companion as you navigate the exciting and ever-evolving world of digital security.

Index

- A
  - Access Control
  - Active Directory
  - Advanced Persistent Threats (APTs)
  - Advanced Penetration Testing Techniques
    - Authentication Bypass
    - Evasion Techniques
    - Exploit Development
    - Man-in-the-Middle (MITM) Attacks
  - Advanced Scapy Topics
    - Custom Layer Fields
    - Fragmenting IP Packets
    - Packet Crafting
    - Packet Injection

- Basics
- Benefits
- Core Components
- Installation
- Interactive Shell
- Layers
- Troubleshooting
- Scripting (Python for Automation)
- Security Audits
- Security Automation and Orchestration (SOAR)